THE VEGAN BOULANGERIE

The best of traditional French baking... egg and dairy-free

Marianne & Jean-Michel

Order this book online at www.trafford.com
or email orders@trafford.com

Most Trafford titles are also available at major online book retailers.

Printed in Victoria, BC, Canada.

ISBN: 978-1-4269-2659-4 (sc)

*Our mission is to efficiently provide the world's finest, most comprehensive book publishing
service, enabling every author to experience success. To find out how to publish your book,
your way, and have it available worldwide, visit us online at www.trafford.com*

Trafford rev. 01/13/2010

www.trafford.com

North America & international
toll-free: 1 888 232 4444 (USA & Canada)
phone: 250 383 6864 ♦ fax: 812 355 4082

The authors would like to thank the following French bakeries:
Pains Tradition à l'Ancienne "Le Four à Bois", Saint-Dizier, France.
Boulangerie Pâtisserie Viennoiserie Thely Philippe, Roanne, France.
Merci!

The authors would also like to thank Animal Aid, Kent, UK, for helping them take the extra step and become vegans.

CONTENTS

Doughs and Crèmes

Coffee Time

Tea-Time Treats

Savoury Pastries   81

Desserts   99

INTRODUCTION

France is renowned for its food all over the world and this includes its baking. The huge appeal of French baking is shown by words like *croissants*, *pains au chocolat*, *quiches* or *gâteau* being commonly used in English, while the famous *baguette* has made its way into people's everyday life and is on offer daily in many bakeries and supermarkets internationally. However, people who have visited France often say that the imported recipes bear no comparison to the original ones. Why? Probably because the French take so much pride in their traditional recipes and attention to detail often has turned baking into an art form in itself. Taste and appearance are not enough to encompass the success criteria for a French bread or pastry. French bakers look for texture and feel, colour, fragrance, the perfect marriage of flavours.

It is no wonder that the French themselves still rely on their local bakery. In fact, even the smallest village in France has at least one bakery and town and city centres have one in almost every street. Display is very important and once again no detail is overlooked. Warm lighting often helps create an inviting atmosphere and shop windows are usually decorated with rural motifs that celebrate the origins of bread: windmills, wheat ears and bags of flour or fields of wild flowers. Traditional French bakers especially take great pride in their work and showcase their art in their shops, where customers can watch bread being prepared and baked in the large wood-fired brick oven.

Most bakeries are boulangeries-pâtisseries, meaning that they provide both bread as well as pastries and cakes, and even exclusive boulangeries offer at least a small range of classic pastries. In addition to bread, pastries and cakes, some French bakeries also sell hand-made chocolates. Most boulangeries-pâtisseries are organised in a similar way: a vast array of breads, including several types of baguette, loaves and wreaths lies in wooden racks at the back of the shop, behind the counter. Pastries and sandwiches are on display under glass around the counter, grouped in savoury and sweet and divided into sections. As for cakes, a selection of what is on offer is displayed in the shop while cakes for special occasions are made on request. Boulangeries-pâtisseries which also sell chocolates will often have them on display in a separate corner of the shop and all boulangeries-pâtisseries have of course a few sweets that children come and buy -along with their *goûter* (afternoon light meal)- on their way home from school. In France people from all social groups go to their local boulangerie at least once a day, whether it is for their daily supply of fresh bread, an easy lunchtime option or a dessert for a special event.

Veganism was almost unheard of in France until a few years ago, but more and more people are becoming aware of the need to cut off animal products from their diet on ethical, environmental or health grounds. Traditional French baking does rely heavily on eggs and dairy, but luckily these can always be replaced by healthier, cruelty-free alternatives. Crème pâtissière without milk or choux pastry without eggs? As the French themselves say, *impossible n'est pas français*: impossible is not a French word!

EQUIPMENT, INGREDIENTS AND TECHNIQUES

Equipment

In traditional French baking some specialities require special moulds or tins. In fact many of these have been created for one specific recipe. We have indicated when and how special equipment should be used, although most of the recipes in this book can be prepared with basic utensils. Specialised baking equipment will produce more authentic baked goods and some pastries depend a lot on their shape. The shell-shaped *madeleines* for example would not be *madeleines* if baked in a muffin pan and the tall fluted *brioche* baked in a cake tin would only be a rich sweet dough bread.

<u>Barquettes moulds</u>: fluted boat-shaped moulds for small tartlet-style pastries.

<u>Bread knife</u>: the appearance and presentation of bread, cakes or pastries when served depend largely on the quality of the knife with which you cut them. A very sharp bread knife will cut neat slices and wedges without breaking the crumb.

<u>Brioche mould</u>: a tall, cylindrical mould with deeply fluted sides.

<u>Candy and deep-fry thermometer</u>: a key item in the preparation of caramels and *beignets*. If you do not have a thermometer, do a test with a small quantity of dough before frying an entire batch of *beignets*. For caramel, drop a spoonful onto a piece of greased aluminium foil. The caramel should harden quickly and remain clear. It should not be fudgey.

Madeleines moulds: *madeleines* are soft sponge cakes from the north-east of France. They come in two different shapes: the classic and most common "*madeleines* de Commercy" are oblong and shell-shaped, while long madeleines look like thick fingers.

Oven thermometer: an indispensable item for baking breads, cakes and pastries. Do not rely on your oven thermostat as there may be a significant difference between the temperature to which you have set the oven and the actual temperature.

Pastry bag: very useful for handling *choux pastry* or piping crèmes into delicate swirls. At a pinch you can make a disposable pastry bag for piping crèmes by turning a square of baking paper into a pouch. Fill with crème and cut a hole in the bottom of the pouch.

Ingredients

Arrowroot: this excellent vegetable thickener can be found in the home baking section of supermarkets.

Capers: the pickled flower buds of a Mediterranean bush.

"Cheese": cheese is used extensively in French cuisine and vegan alternatives are particularly suited for baking. Try the smooth and creamy spreads as part of a classic *tartine* meal, "cheddar-style" slices melted in *croque-monsieurs*, and grated "parmesan" for sprinkling.

Harissa: a popular spicy paste brought to France by the immigrants from North Africa.

Herbes de Provence: a mixture of dried thyme, basil, rosemary and bay leaf. These herbs are widely used in Mediterranean specialities.

Margarine: both hard and soft vegan margarines are used in this book, which are readily available from the dairy section of supermarkets.

Marzipan: this thick almond paste is popular with French bakers, as a filling or garnish. When buying marzipan, always make sure that it does not contain egg.

Pain au levain: bread made with levain. Levain is a sourdough used in the preparation of some wholemeal breads. It is prepared by leaving yeast dough to ferment for three days.

Pâte à choux: choux pastry. This is the basic pastry for *éclairs*, *croque-en-bouche* and other desserts.

Pâte brisée: shortcrust pastry. *Pâte brisée* is used for savoury tarts, pies and individual pastries.

Pâte feuilletée: puff pastry. *Pâte feuilletée* is used a lot in French baking and for both sweet and savoury pastries. As making it is not easy, ready-made puff pastry can be used. Vegan versions are available in most supermarkets.

Pâte levée: *pâte levée* is a leavened dough using yeast, mostly used in the preparation of sweet pastries and desserts. However, it is very versatile and by using less sugar it can be the base for savoury pastries.

Pâte levée feuilletée: *pâte levée feuilletée* is puff pastry made with leavened dough. Although it takes a little longer to prepare, the result is worth the effort. Pastries will be both soft and delicately crisp. All recipes using pâte levée feuilletée can also be made with ordinary puff pastry.

Pâte sablée: a sweetenened type of shortcrust pastry. *Pâte sablée* is commonly used for sweet biscuits and tarts. For quicker recipes using *pâte sablée*, ready-made shortcrust pastry can also be used.

Polenta: a fine yellow cornmeal used in Italy and Southern France in cooking and baking.

Pralin: nuts caramelised in boiling syrup. Pralin can be used as a filling, garnish or topping and can be prepared with any type of nuts.

Soya mince: textured vegetable protein can be bought frozen or dry. The frozen version is darker and has a stronger flavour. The dry "mince" comes in various forms, from small granules to big chunks.

Tapenade: a popular spread from the Mediterranean, *tapenade* is a paste made from puréed olives, capers and garlic.

Tofu: one of the most versatile ingredients. We have used silken-style, extra firm and braised tofu, which can all be found in the Asian food or free-from/vegetarian section of most supermarkets.

Wine: Most wines are clarified using gelatine or egg, so it is a good idea to check that the wine is vegan suitable.

Yeast: a key ingredient in French baking. Most leavened doughs use yeast and not chemical leaveners. Easy-bake dry yeast is used in this book. Always work in a draught-free room when using yeast. Make sure that the liquid is not too warm when mixing it to the flour and yeast.

Tips and Techniques

Baking blind: baking the pastry before adding the filling. This is done by covering the dough with a layer of ceramic beads and will prevent the pastry from blistering.

Fermentation: the biological and chemical actions taking place as the bread ages and rises.

Kneading: working the dough by pressing on it, then folding over and pressing with the heel of the hand. Kneading helps the formation of gluten which gives the bread its shape and plays an important role in the rising process.

Pastry: to lift delicate uncooked pastry such as *pâte sablée* or *pâte brisée* into a tart tin, simply wrap the rolled out pastry around the rolling pin and then unroll the pastry carefully over the tin.

Preparation: when preparing a recipe, always try to have as much equipment and ingredients ready before you start so everything goes smoothly. Weighing all the ingredients and having them at hand makes things easier. Also, having the cake tins and baking sheets already greased and/or floured before it is time to put the dough or pastries in will help. Remember to preheat the oven.

Retarding: slowing down the growth of the yeast with refrigeration. Generally, a long, slow fermentation makes for better flavour and texture in breads.

Swirl: to pipe choux pastry into a nice swirling puff pipe a spiral, starting with the middle and expanding into a round flat base, then start piping up, this time going from the edge towards the middle.

BREAD

Introduction

Bread is an important part of every French meal. You will always find a basket of fresh bread on the table, or a warm, crisp *baguette* ready to be shared. Serving bread is in itself something of a social ritual. Some people will never use a knife and insist on tearing the bread into pieces with their hands, while others make a point of cutting equally-sized slices as a mark of respect for all guests. Most French people buy fresh bread every day, sometimes twice a day. Baguettes and other sticks are stored at room temperature in a paper or cloth bag. Day-old bread can be drizzled with water and warmed through in a hot oven for 5 minutes.

Despite the increasing popularity of bread machines and the myriad other specialty breads, sticks and loaves on offer in French *boulangeries,* the classic baguette remains the firm favourite, and it is quite common to see people carrying home armfuls of baguettes in the early morning. There is nothing quite like eating a baguette straight from the oven, when it is still warm and crisp. In fact, its appeal is so huge among the French that they all know from experience that a good baguette will never reach home intact. This has almost become a saying in France and some bakers display a cartoon with that message in their shop windows. Other popular sticks include the thinner *ficelle* and *pain épi*, a crisp, wholemeal bread baked in the shape of a wheat ear as a symbol of the social significance of bread. Each region has its own variations, from *pain noir*, the black buckwheat flour bread of Brittany, to the Provençal *fougasse* and the Alsatian *pretzel*. Local and seasonal cereals, herbs or vegetables can also be added to produce interesting flavours.

Beside being served as an accompaniment, bread is often used as the basis for an informal meal, from sandwiches and Mediterranean *pan bagnat* to *tartines* of patés and spreads and toasted *croque-monsieur*. Leftover stale bread can be turned into *pain perdu*, or "lost bread", to provide a quick and easy dessert.

When using yeast it is necessary to work in a draught-free, relatively warm room for the dough to rise effectively. Do not speed up the fermentation process by leaving the dough in a hot place. When yeast grows slowly you get the richer, fuller flavour of breads made with retarded dough. Bread made with *levain,* or sourdough, keep fresh longer, but its preparation can be quite time consuming, so it is worth making large quantities. Always check that the bread is fully baked. Gently tap the underside of the loaf: it should sound hollow. Also, a knife or skewer should come out clean.

Baguette

(makes 2)
500g/1lb2oz white bread flour
1 tablespoon dry yeast
1 tablespoon caster sugar
1 teaspoon salt
350ml/12fl.oz lukewarm water
Extra white flour

1. Mix the flour, salt, sugar and yeast in a large mixing bowl, form a well in the centre and pour in the water.
2. Combine with a wooden spoon, then knead for 3 minutes.
3. Cover with a cloth and leave to rise for 2 hours in a warm place.
4. Turn the dough out onto a floured surface and knead well. The dough should be quite firm; add a little flour if it is too soft.
5. Divide the dough in two and roll each half to form a stick of about 4cm/1½inch diameter. Transfer to a floured baking sheet and taper both ends of each baguette.
6. With a sharp knife make deep diagonal cuts at regular intervals in the top of the dough. Also score the sticks slightly along both sides.
7. Leave to rise for a further 30 minutes.
8. Preheat the oven to 200°C/400°F/Gas mark 6 and place a small oven-proof dish filled with hot water on the bottom shelf.
9. Brush the dough with water and bake for 25-30 minutes.
10. Rub the baguettes with a little flour while still hot.

Ficelle

(makes 3 thin sticks)
250g/9oz white bread flour
1 teaspoon dry yeast
1 tablespoon caster sugar
½ teaspoon salt
175ml/6fl.oz lukewarm water

1. Mix the flour, salt, sugar and yeast in a large mixing bowl, form a well in the centre and pour in the water.
2. Stir with a wooden spoon, then knead for 3 minutes. Add a little flour if the dough is sticky.
3. Cover with a cloth and leave to rise for 2 hours in a warm place.
4. Turn the dough out onto a floured surface, sprinkle with flour and knead. Divide it into three equal portions. Roll each one into a long stick with rounded ends of approximately 2cm/¾inch diameter and transfer to a floured baking sheet.
5. With a sharp knife cut the sticks slightly along both sides.
6. Leave them to rise for a further 30 minutes.
7. Preheat the oven to 200°C/400°F/Gas mark 6.
8. Brush the ficelles with water, sprinkle with a little flour and bake for 20 minutes.

Petits Pains

Petits pains are delicious served warm, cut open along one side and spread thinly with vegan margarine and jam.

(makes 12)
500g/1lb2oz white bread flour
1 tablespoon dry yeast
2 tablespoons caster sugar
1 teaspoon salt
325ml/11fl.oz lukewarm water

1. Sift together the flour, salt and sugar into a large mixing bowl. Mix in the yeast, form a well in the centre and pour in the water.
2. Combine with a wooden spoon, then knead for 3 minutes.
3. Cover with a cloth and leave to rise for 2 hours in a warm place.
4. Turn the dough out onto a floured surface and knead again. Add a little flour if it is too soft. Roll the dough into a stick and then slice it into 12 equal portions. Roll each one into a small stick approximately 13cm/5inch long and transfer to a floured baking sheet.
5. With a knife score each roll slightly along one side.
6. Leave to rise for a further 30 minutes.
7. Preheat the oven to 200°C/400°F/Gas mark 6 and place a small oven-proof dish filled with hot water on the bottom shelf.
8. Brush the rolls with water and bake for 20 minutes.

Pain de Mie

(makes 2 small loaves)
500g/1lb2oz white bread flour
1 tablespoon dry yeast
1 tablespoon caster sugar
1 teaspoon salt
350ml/12fl.oz lukewarm water
Vegan soft margarine

1. Sift together the flour, salt and sugar into a large mixing bowl. Mix in the yeast, form a well in the centre and pour in the water.
2. Combine with a wooden spoon, then knead for 1 minute.
3. Cover with a cloth and leave to rise for 2 hours in a warm place.
4. Sprinkle with a little flour and knead again.
5. Divide the dough in two and transfer each half into a medium-size floured loaf tin (approximately 1litre/2pint capacity).

6. Leave to rise for a further 30 minutes.
7. Preheat the oven to 200°C/400°F/Gas mark 6.
8. Brush the top of the loaves with margarine and bake for 25-30 minutes until a knife or skewer comes out clean. Transfer to a cooling rack.

Pain Épi

(makes 1 large stick)
200g/7oz wholemeal bread flour
200g/7oz plain flour
1 rounded tablespoon dry yeast
1 tablespoon caster sugar
½ teaspoon salt
300ml/10fl.oz water

1. Mix together the wholemeal flour, plain flour, sugar, salt and yeast into a large mixing bowl, form a well in the centre and pour in the water.
2. Combine with a wooden spoon, then knead for 5 minutes.
3. Cover with a cloth and put in the fridge. Leave overnight so fermentation is slow.
4. Turn the dough out onto a floured surface and knead again. Roll into a stick approximately 40cm/16inch long and transfer to a floured baking sheet.
5. With scissors make about 5 cuts at regular interval on either side of the stick, alternating sides. The pain épi should look like a wheat ear.
6. Leave to rise for 30 minutes in a warm place.
7. Preheat the oven to 200°C/400°F/Gas Mark 6.
8. Rub a little white flour over the stick and bake for 30-35 minutes.

Soft Soya Bread

(makes 1 loaf)
200g/7oz white bread flour
50g/2oz soya flour
1 teaspoon dry yeast
½ tablespoon baking powder
½ tablespoon caster sugar
½ teaspoon salt
175ml/6fl.oz lukewarm water

1. Sift together the white flour, soya flour, salt and sugar into a large mixing bowl. Stir in the yeast and baking powder, form a well in the centre and pour in the water.
2. Combine with a wooden spoon, then knead for 3 minutes. Add a little flour if the dough is sticky.
3. Cover with a cloth and put in the fridge. Leave overnight so fermentation is slow.
4. Turn the dough out onto a floured surface and knead well. Roll into a large circle. Roll up; moisten the edge with water and seal. Taper both ends.
5. Place the loaf, seam side down, on a baking sheet lined with baking paper. Make shallow lattice cuts in the top of the dough.
6. Leave to rise for a further 30 minutes.
7. Preheat the oven to 175°C/350°F/Gas mark 4 and place a small oven-proof dish filled with hot water on the bottom shelf.
8. Brush the loaf with water and bake for 30 minutes.

Levain

This sourdough is used for the "pains au *levain*": *pain de campagne* and *bâtard*. Because it needs to be made three days in advance it is easiest to make enough for two breads. You can reduce the quantities below if you only want to make one bread using *levain*. With regular water and flour feeds, any remaining *levain* can also be kept in the fridge for up to a week. Just mix 30g/1oz bread flour and 50ml/2fl.oz water into the *levain* every day. Pains "au *levain*" keep fresh longer and take longer to bake.

(makes 200g/7oz *levain*)
75g/3oz white bread flour
1 level tablespoon dry yeast
125ml/4½fl.oz lukewarm water

1. In a mixing bowl, whisk together the dry yeast and the water until the yeast has dissolved.
2. Add the flour gradually by sprinkling it in the water and then whisking together.
3. When no large lumps remain cover with cling film, make a few holes in the film with a fork and leave at room temperature for 3 days.
4. Mix well before use.

Pain de Campagne

(makes 1 large loaf)
600g/1lb5oz plain flour
300g/10oz rye flour
100g/4oz *levain* (see above)
2 tablespoons dry yeast
2 teaspoons salt
400ml/14fl.oz lukewarm water

1. Mix together the plain flour, rye flour, salt and yeast in a large mixing bowl, form a well in the centre and pour in the water and levain.
2. Combine with a wooden spoon, then knead for 3 minutes.
3. Cover with a cloth and leave to rise overnight.
4. The next day knead again well. Add a little flour if the dough becomes too sticky. Roll into a large oblong loaf.
5. With a sharp knife make diagonal cuts at regular intervals in the top of the dough. Transfer to a floured baking sheet.
6. Leave the loaf to rise for 3 hours.
7. Preheat the oven to 190°C/375°F/Gas mark 5 and place a small oven-proof dish filled with hot water on the bottom shelf.
8. Bake for 55-60 minutes. Check that the bread is fully baked by tapping the underside of the loaf: it should sound hollow.

Bâtard

(makes 1 large loaf)
700g/1lb9oz brown bread flour
150g/5oz rye flour
100g/4oz *levain* (see above)
1 rounded tablespoon dry yeast
1 teaspoon salt
400ml/14fl.oz lukewarm water

1. Mix the bread flour, rye flour, yeast and salt into a large mixing bowl, form a well in the centre and pour in the levain and water.
2. Combine with a wooden spoon, then knead until smooth.
3. Cover with a cloth and leave to rise overnight.
4. Turn the dough out onto a floured surface and knead well. Roll into a large round loaf and transfer to a floured baking sheet.
5. Leave to rise for 3 hours.
6. Preheat the oven to 190°C/375°F/Gas mark 5 and place a small oven-proof dish filled with hot water on the bottom shelf.
7. Bake the loaf for 55 minutes. Check that the bread is fully baked by tapping the underside of the loaf: it should sound hollow.

Bread Crumbs

Breadcrumbs will keep in a tin for a long time and are great for coating vegetable burgers or for thickening sauces. Larger crumbs make an excellent vegetable "mince".

Any type of leftover bread

1. Crumb the bread very finely in a food processor.
2. Place the crumbs in a large baking tray and leave in a hot oven until brown and completely dry, shaking the tray regularly.
3. Take out of the oven and leave the crumbs in the tray to cool before transferring to a tin.

Sweet Dough Baguette

Sweet dough bread, also called "Pain Viennois," is used in both sweet and savoury recipes. It is perfect dipped in a hot chocolate or coffee but will also make great sandwiches.

(makes 1)
200g/7oz plain flour
50g/2oz rice flour
1 tablespoon dry yeast
2 tablespoons caster sugar
1 teaspoon salt
35g/1½oz soft vegan margarine
125ml/4½fl.oz lukewarm soya milk, unsweetened

1. Sift the plain flour and rice flour into a large mixing bowl and form a well in the centre.
2. Mix the yeast with 1 tablespoon sugar and a little soya milk. Pour into the well and sprinkle with a little flour.
3. Cover with a cloth and leave in a warm place for 10 minutes.
4. Mix in the remaining soya milk, 1 tablespoon sugar, the margarine and salt. Combine and knead firmly.
5. Cover with a cloth and leave to rise for 50 minutes in a warm place.
6. Turn the dough out onto a floured surface and knead again. Roll into a stick approximately 4cm/1½inch thick and transfer to a baking sheet lined with baking paper.
7. Leave at room temperature for 30 minutes.
8. Preheat the oven to 190°C/375°F/Gas mark 5.
9. Brush the dough with a little water and bake for 20 minutes.

Sweet Dough Rolls

Sweet dough rolls, buns and baguettes

(makes 8)
400g/14oz plain flour
100g/4oz rice flour
1 rounded tablespoon dry yeast
3 tablespoons caster sugar
1 teaspoon salt
75g/3oz soft vegan margarine
Melted margarine for brushing
250ml/9fl.oz lukewarm soya milk, unsweetened

1. Sift the plain flour and rice flour into a large mixing bowl and form a well in the centre.
2. Mix the yeast with 1 tablespoon sugar and a little soya milk. Pour into the well and sprinkle with a little flour.
3. Cover with a cloth and leave in a warm place for 10 minutes.
4. Mix in the remaining soya milk, 2 tablespoons sugar, the margarine and salt. Combine and knead firmly.
5. Cover with a cloth and leave to rise for 50 minutes in a warm place.
6. Turn the dough out onto a floured surface and knead again. Roll into a stick and slice it into 8 equal portions. Shape each portion into a round roll and transfer to a baking sheet lined with baking paper.
7. Brush with a little melted margarine and leave at room temperature for 30 minutes.
8. Preheat the oven to 190°C/375°F/Gas mark 5.
9. Brush the rolls with a little water and bake for 15-20 minutes.

Crusty Seed Baguette

(makes 1)
250g/9oz white bread flour
1 tablespoon dry yeast
50g/2oz sunflower seeds
50g/2oz pumpkin seeds
15g/½oz sesame seeds
½ tablespoon caster sugar
¼ teaspoon salt
150ml/5fl.oz lukewarm water

1. In a large mixing bowl, mix the flour, yeast, salt and sugar.
2. Add in the sunflower seeds and pumpkin seeds, form a well in the centre and pour in the water.
3. Combine with a wooden spoon, then knead for 3 minutes.
4. Cover with a cloth and leave to rise for 2 hours in a warm place.
5. Turn the dough out onto a floured surface and knead well. Add a little flour if it is too soft. Roll into a stick of about 4cm/1½inch diameter and transfer to a floured baking sheet.
6. Brush the dough with water and roll in the sesame seeds.
7. With a knife make diagonal cuts at regular intervals in the top of the dough. Also score the baguette slightly along both sides.
8. Leave to rise for a further 30 minutes.
9. Preheat the oven to 200°C/400°F/Gas mark 6 and place a small oven-proof dish filled with hot water on the bottom shelf. Wait for 2 minutes.
10. Spray the inside walls of the oven with water and immediately bake the baguette for 25 minutes. Watch out for the steam when spraying inside the oven.

Tomato and Herb Roulé

(makes 1 medium loaf)
250g/9oz white bread flour
1 teaspoon dry yeast
1 tablespoon caster sugar
1 teaspoon salt
175ml/6fl.oz lukewarm water
2 tablespoons tomato purée
3 tablespoons herbes de Provence
Olive oil

1. Sift together the flour, salt and sugar into a large mixing bowl. Mix in the yeast and form a well in the centre.
2. Mix the tomato purée and water and pour into the well.
3. Combine with a wooden spoon, then knead for 1 minute.

4. Cover with a cloth and leave to rise for 2 hours in a warm place.
5. Turn the dough out onto a floured surface and knead firmly. Roll out into a large square. Brush with a little olive oil and sprinkle the herbs all over. Roll up, moisten the edge with water and seal.
6. Place the loaf, seam side down, in a medium-size loaf tin (approximately 1 litre/2pint capacity) lined with baking paper.
7. Leave to rise for a further 30 minutes.
8. Preheat the oven to 175°C/350°F/Gas mark 4 .
9. Bake the loaf for 30 minutes and transfer to a cooling rack.

Poppy Seed Baguette

Poppy seed bread is delicious spread thinly with vegan margarine and soft vegan cheese.

Loaf "au levain", poppy seed baguette and soft soya bread.

(makes 1)
250g/9oz white bread flour
1 teaspoon dry yeast
1 teaspoon salt
175ml/6fl.oz lukewarm water
25g/1oz poppy seeds

1. Mix the flour, yeast and salt in a large mixing bowl, form a well in the centre and pour in the water.
2. Combine with a wooden spoon, then knead for 3 minutes.
3. Cover with a cloth and leave to rise for 2 hours in a warm place.
4. Turn the dough out onto a floured surface and knead well. Roll into a stick of approximately 4cm/1½inch diameter.
5. Spread a little water all over the dough and roll the stick in the poppy seeds. Transfer to a lightly greased baking sheet.
6. With a sharp knife score the baguette slightly along both sides.
7. Leave to rise for a further 30 minutes.
8. Preheat the oven to 200°C/400°F/Gas mark 6 and place a small oven-proof dish filled with hot water on the bottom shelf.
9. Bake the baguette for 25 minutes.

Multi-Flavoured Wreath

(serves 7)
500g/1lb2oz white bread flour
1 tablespoon dry yeast
1 tablespoon caster sugar
1 teaspoon salt
125ml/4½fl.oz lukewarm water
175ml/6fl.oz lukewarm rice milk
For garnish:
1 tablespoon wheat germ
1 tablespoon linseed
1 tablespoon cumin seeds
1 tablespoon sesame seeds
1 tablespoon poppy seeds
1 tablespoon crushed pistachios
1 tablespoon grated vegan parmesan

1. Sift together the flour, sugar and salt into a large mixing bowl. Mix in the yeast, form a well in the centre and pour in the water and rice milk.
2. Combine, then knead firmly.
3. Cover with a cloth and leave to rise for 2 hours in a warm place.
4. Turn the dough out onto a lightly floured surface and knead well. Roll the dough into a stick and slice it into 7 equal portions.
5. Roll each one into a round roll and place the rolls into a wreath on a large floured baking sheet.
6. Brush with a little water and sprinkle each roll in the wreath with one of the ingredients for garnish.
7. Leave to rise for a further 30 minutes.
8. Preheat the oven to 200°C/400°F/Gas mark 6.
9. Bake for 30 minutes.

Linseed Bread

(makes 1 loaf)
500g/1lb2oz white bread flour
1 tablespoon dry yeast
1 tablespoon caster sugar
1 teaspoon salt
350ml/12fl.oz lukewarm water
100g/4oz linseed
Extra linseed
Linseed oil for brushing

1. Sift together the flour, salt and sugar into a large mixing bowl. Mix in the yeast and linseed, form a well in the centre and pour in the water.
2. Combine with a wooden spoon, then knead well.
3. Cover with a cloth and leave to rise for 2 hours in a warm place.
4. Sprinkle with a little flour and knead again.
5. Transfer the dough into a large cake tin (approximately 1½litre/2½pint capacity) brushed with a little linseed oil.
6. Leave to rise for a further 30 minutes.
7. Preheat the oven to 200°C/400°F/Gas mark 6.
8. Brush the loaf with a little linseed oil and sprinkle with linseed. Bake for 30-35 minutes and transfer to a cooling rack.

Brown Onion Bread

(makes 1 loaf)
500g/1lb2oz brown bread flour
1 tablespoon dry yeast
½ teaspoon salt
300ml/10fl.oz lukewarm water
200g/7oz onions, chopped
25g/1oz vegan margarine
1 tablespoon French mustard
1 teaspoon yellow mustard seeds
Pinch of sugar

1. Put the onions and the margarine in a pan. Fry the onions until soft and brown. Remove from the heat, add a pinch of sugar and stir well. Set aside to cool.
2. Mix together the flour, yeast and salt into a large mixing bowl, form a well in the centre and pour in the water.
3. Add in the onion, mustard and mustard seeds.
4. Combine with a wooden spoon, then knead.
5. Cover with a cloth and leave to rise for 2 hours in a warm place.
6. Sprinkle with a little flour and knead again.
7. Transfer the dough into a large, slightly greased and floured loaf tin (approximately 1½litre/2½pint capacity).
8. Leave to rise for a further 30 minutes.
9. Preheat the oven to 200°C/400°F/Gas mark 6.
10. Brush the loaf with water and bake for 35-40 minutes until a knife comes out clean. Transfer to a cooling rack.

Carrot Bread

(makes 1 large loaf)
500g/1lb2oz plain flour
1 tablespoon dry yeast
1 teaspoon baking powder
1 tablespoon caster sugar
1 tablespoon canola oil
1 teaspoon salt
1 teaspoon paprika
½ teaspoon cinnamon
300ml/10fl.oz lukewarm water
200g/8oz carrots, peeled and grated

1. Sift together the flour, salt and sugar into a large mixing bowl. Mix in the yeast, baking powder, paprika and cinnamon.
2. Form a well in the centre and pour in the water and canola oil. Add in the grated carrots.
3. Combine with a wooden spoon, then knead quickly.
4. Cover with a cloth and leave to rise for 2 hours in a warm place.
5. Knead again, adding flour until the dough just comes together.
6. Transfer the dough into a large, greased and floured cake tin (approximately 2litre/3½pint capacity) .
7. Leave to rise for a further 30 minutes.
8. Preheat the oven to 200°C/400°F/Gas mark 6.
9. Bake for 40 minutes until a skewer or knife comes out clean. Transfer to a cooling rack.

Pepper Bread

(makes 1 loaf)
500g/1lb2oz plain flour
1 tablespoon dry yeast
1 tablespoon baking powder
1 tablespoon caster sugar
1 teaspoon salt
250ml/9fl.oz lukewarm water
1 tablespoon extra virgin olive oil
½ red pepper
½ yellow pepper
½ green pepper
1 plump garlic clove, crushed
Extra olive oil

1. Sift together the flour, salt and sugar into a large mixing bowl. Mix in the yeast, form a well in the centre and pour in the water and olive oil.

2. Process the peppers and garlic and put in the well. Combine with a wooden spoon.
3. Cover with a cloth and leave to rise for 2 hours in a warm place.
4. Sprinkle with a little flour and knead quickly.
5. Transfer the dough into a large cake tin (approximately 1½litre/2½pint capacity) brushed with a little olive oil.
6. Leave to rise for a further 30 minutes.
7. Preheat the oven to 200°C/400°F/Gas mark 6.
8. Brush the loaf with a little olive oil and bake for 35-40 minutes until a knife or skewer comes out clean. Transfer to a cooling rack.

Fruit and Nut Rolls

(makes 12)
500g/1lb2oz plain flour
1 tablespoon dry yeast
1 tablespoon caster sugar
1 tablespoon vegetable oil
1 teaspoon salt
325ml/11fl.oz lukewarm water
50g/2oz dried apricots, coarsely chopped
50g/2oz prunes, coarsely chopped
50g/2oz chopped hazelnuts
50g/2oz chopped almonds
50g/2oz chopped walnuts
25g/1oz chopped pine nuts

1. Place half of the hazelnuts, almonds, walnuts and pine nuts in a tray under a hot grill until brown and fragrant, shaking the tray now and then to ensure even browning. Mix well and set aside to cool.
2. Mix together the flour, yeast, sugar and salt into a large mixing bowl.
3. Put the apricots and prunes in another bowl with the grilled nuts and mix well. Add to the flour mixture.
4. Form a well in the centre and pour in the water and vegetable oil. Combine with a wooden spoon, then knead for 1 minute.
5. Cover with a cloth and leave to rise for 2 hours in a warm place.
6. Turn the dough out onto a floured surface and knead well. Roll the dough into a stick and then slice it into 12 equal portions. Pat the slices into round rolls and lay them flat on a floured baking sheet.

7. Drizzle with a little water. Sprinkle the remaining nuts on the rolls and press the nuts into the dough.
8. Leave to rise for a further 30 minutes.
9. Preheat the oven to 200°C/400°F/Gas mark 6.
10. Bake the rolls for 20 minutes.

Quick Raisin Bread

(makes 1 loaf)
500g/1lb2oz plain flour
4 tablespoons baking powder
1 teaspoon salt
300ml/10fl.oz water
50ml/2fl.oz soya milk, unsweetened
2 rounded tablespoons granulated sugar
2 rounded tablespoons vegan soft margarine
50g/2oz sultanas
50g/2oz currants

1. Cream the margarine and sugar in a mixing bowl until light and fluffy.
2. Sift together the flour, salt and baking powder into a large mixing bowl. Mix in the sultanas and currants.
3. Form a well in the centre and pour in the water and soya milk. Also add the creamed margarine.
4. Combine quickly with a wooden spoon.
5. Transfer the dough into a lightly greased and floured cake tin (approximately 1½litre/2½pint capacity).
6. Bake in a preheated oven at 200°C/400°F/Gas mark 6 for 35 minutes until a skewer or knife comes out clean. Transfer to a cooling rack.

Quick Corn Bread

(makes 1 loaf)
300g/10oz plain flour
100g/4oz polenta
150g/5oz sweetcorn kernels
3 tablespoons baking powder
1 tablespoon caster sugar
1 teaspoon salt
225ml/8fl.oz water
1 tablespoon corn oil
Extra corn oil
Polenta for sprinkling

1. Sift together the plain flour, polenta, baking powder, sugar and salt into a large mixing bowl.
2. Form a well in the centre and pour in the water and corn oil. Also add in the sweet corn.
3. Combine with a wooden spoon.
4. Transfer the dough into a large cake tin (approximately 1½litre/2½pint capacity) brushed with a little corn oil and sprinkled with polenta.
5. Place a small oven-proof dish filled with hot water on the bottom shelf of the oven.
6. Bake in a preheated oven at 200°C/400°F/Gas mark 6 for 35-40 minutes until a skewer or knife comes out clean.

Alsatian Pretzel

Traditional *pretzels* are different from the salted snack biscuits with which the word "pretzel" is often associated. They have a soft texture like bread, are much bigger and are sold fresh in Alsatians bakeries as an individual snack or light meal.

(makes 8)
500g/1lb2oz white bread flour
½ teaspoon salt
2 tablespoons dry yeast
325ml/11fl.oz lukewarm water
1 tablespoon salt crystals
Extra salt crystals

1. Sift the flour and salt into a large mixing bowl. Mix in the yeast, form a well in the centre and pour in the water.
2. Combine with a wooden spoon, then knead for 3 minutes.
3. Cover with a cloth and leave to rise for 2 hours in a warm place.
4. Turn the dough out onto a floured surface and knead well. Roll the dough into a stick and then slice it into 8 equal portions. Roll each one into a very long sausage approximately 65cm/26inch long.
5. For each stick, start by forming a heart shape, joining both ends in the centre. Twist the ends together and dampen with water before tucking them under the bottom half of the pretzel (each end pointing to the opposite direction). Transfer to a floured baking sheet.
6. Dissolve the salt crystals in a little boiling water and set aside.
7. Leave the pretzels to rise for 15 minutes.
8. Preheat the oven to 190°C/375°F/Gas mark 5.

9. Brush the salty water over the pretzels and sprinkle lightly with salt crystals.
10. Place a small oven-proof dish filled with hot water on the bottom shelf of the oven. Wait for 2 minutes.
11. Spray the inside walls of the oven with water and immediately bake the pretzels for 15 minutes. Watch out for the steam when spraying inside the oven.

Olive Fougasse

(serves 4-6)
300g/10oz plain flour
1 tablespoon dry yeast
½ teaspoon salt
5 tablespoons extra virgin olive oil
Extra olive oil
100g/4oz green olives, pitted
100g/4oz black olives, pitted
150ml/5fl.oz lukewarm water

1. Slice half of the green olives and black olives.
2. Put the flour, yeast and salt into a large bowl and mix well.
3. Form a well in the centre and pour in the water and olive oil. Add in both the sliced and whole olives.
4. Combine with a wooden spoon, then knead until the olives are evenly mixed into the dough.
5. Cover with a cloth and leave to rise for 2 hours in a warm place.
6. Sprinkle the dough with a little flour and knead again before turning out onto a surface brushed with a little olive oil. Roll the dough into 8 sticks approximately 1½cm/½inch thick.
7. Brush a baking sheet with olive oil and place 4 sticks of dough 5cm/2inch apart. Put the other sticks across.
8. Brush the fougasse with olive oil and leave to rise for 30 minutes.
9. Preheat the oven to 200°C/400°F/Gas mark 6.
10. Bake for 30-35 minutes. Cut into pieces to serve.

Vegan Parmesan Fougasse

(serves 4)
300g/10oz plain flour
1 tablespoon dry yeast
½ teaspoon salt
1 tablespoon extra virgin olive oil
Extra olive oil
50g/2oz black olives, pitted and chopped

50g/2oz grated vegan parmesan
Extra grated vegan parmesan
175ml/6fl.oz lukewarm water

1. Put the flour, yeast and salt into a large bowl and mix well.
2. Form a well in the centre and pour in the water and olive oil. Add in the chopped olives and grated parmesan.
3. Combine with a wooden spoon, then knead for 1 minute.
4. Cover with a cloth and leave to rise for 2 hours in a warm place.
5. Sprinkle the dough with a little flour and knead again before turning out onto a surface brushed with a little olive oil. Roll the dough into 8 sticks approximately 1½cm/½inch thick.
6. Sprinkle a baking sheet with a little olive oil and place 4 sticks of dough 5cm/2inch apart. Put the other sticks across.
7. Brush the fougasse with olive oil, sprinkle with a little parmesan and leave to rise for 30 minutes.
8. Preheat the oven to 200°C/400°F/Gas mark 6.
9. Bake for 30-35 minutes and cut into pieces to serve.

Vegan Pepperoni Fougasse

(serves 4)
300g/10oz plain flour
1 tablespoon dry yeast
½ teaspoon salt
1 tablespoon extra virgin olive oil
Extra olive oil
50g/2oz shallots, chopped
25g/1oz capers
100g/4oz vegan "pepperoni"
150ml/5fl.oz lukewarm water

1. Gently fry the shallots in the olive oil until soft. Remove from the heat, add in the capers and mix well.
2. Put the flour, yeast and salt into a large bowl and mix well.
3. Form a well in the centre and pour in the water. Add in the shallots and capers.
4. Combine with a wooden spoon, then knead for 1 minute.
5. Cover with a cloth and leave to rise for 2 hours in a warm place.
6. Knead the dough again before turning out onto a floured surface. Form into a large oval (approximately 1cm/½inch thick) and transfer to a greased baking sheet.
7. Cut the vegan "pepperoni" into long thin strips and press them into the dough. Brush the fougasse with olive oil and leave to rise for 30 minutes.
8. Preheat the oven to 200°C/400°F/Gas mark 6.
9. Bake for 25 minutes.

Sundried Tomato Fougassettes

(makes 4)
300g/10oz plain flour
1 tablespoon dry yeast
½ teaspoon salt
5 tablespoons canola oil
Extra canola oil
150g/5oz sundried tomatoes, coarsely chopped
150ml/5fl.oz lukewarm water

1. Put the flour, yeast and salt into a large bowl and mix well.
2. Form a well in the centre and pour in the water and canola oil. Add in the sundried tomatoes.
3. Combine with a wooden spoon, then knead for 1 minute or until the tomatoes are evenly mixed into the dough.
4. Cover with a cloth and leave to rise for 2 hours in a warm place.
5. Knead the dough again before turning out onto a lightly greased surface. Split the dough in 4 and flatten each piece out into an oval shape approximately 1cm/½inch thick.
6. Transfer onto a greased baking sheet.
7. Brush with canola oil and leave to rise for 30 minutes.
8. Preheat the oven to 200°C/400°F/Gas mark 6.
9. Bake the fougassettes for 20-25 minutes.

Crusty Mushroom Fougasse

(serves 4)
300g/10oz plain flour
1 tablespoon dry yeast
½ teaspoon salt
½ teaspoon black pepper
1 tablespoon olive oil
Extra olive oil
200g/7oz fresh mushrooms, finely chopped
50g/2oz onions, finely chopped
150ml/5fl.oz lukewarm water

1. Put the mushrooms and the onions in a pan with the olive oil. Cover and fry gently for 10 minutes. Uncover and fry for 5 more minutes, stirring occasionally. Remove from the heat and set aside.
2. Put the flour, yeast, salt and pepper into a large bowl and mix well, form a well in the centre and pour in the water.
3. Combine with a wooden spoon, then knead for 1 minute.
4. Cover with a cloth and leave to rise for 2 hours in a warm place.

5. Knead the dough again before turning out onto a floured surface. Divide in two and roll each half out into an oval shape approximately ½cm/¼inch thick.

6. Place one of the ovals onto a greased baking sheet and spread out the mushrooms and onions over it, avoiding the edge. Brush the edge with water.

7. Place the other oval on top and seal the edge by pressing with your fingertips. Cut 4 diagonal slits in the top.

8. Brush the fougasse with a little olive oil and leave to rise for 30 minutes.

9. Preheat the oven to 200°C/400°F/Gas mark 6 and place a small oven-proof dish filled with hot water on the bottom shelf. Close the oven and wait for 2 minutes.

10. Spray the inside walls of the oven with water and immediately put the fougasse in the oven. Watch out for the steam when spraying inside the oven. Bake for 25 minutes and transfer to a cooling rack.

Fougasse Mosaic

(serves 4-6)
300g/10oz plain flour
1 tablespoon dry yeast
½ teaspoon salt
2 tablespoons extra virgin olive oil
Extra olive oil
25g/1oz yellow pepper, finely chopped
25g/1oz fresh tomato, finely chopped
25g/1oz black pitted olives, sliced
25g/1oz capers
175ml/6fl.oz lukewarm water

1. Put the flour, yeast and salt into a large mixing bowl and mix well, form a well in the centre and pour in the water and olive oil.
2. Combine with a wooden spoon, then knead for 1 minute.
3. Cover with a cloth and leave to rise for 2 hours in a warm place.
4. Knead the dough again before turning out onto a floured surface. Shape the dough into a stick and slice it into 8 equal portions.
5. Roll each portion into a ball and flatten out with the palm of the hand. For each one, press into the dough half of the peppers, or tomatoes, or green olives or black olives.
6. Transfer the coloured pieces onto a greased baking sheet, setting them tightly close to each other into an oval and pressing with you hands to flatten the dough. Avoid putting 2 pieces with the same ingredient next to each other so that the colours are evenly spread out.
7. Brush the fougasse with olive oil and leave to rise for 30 minutes.
8. Preheat the oven to 200°C/400°F/Gas mark 6.
9. Bake for 25 minutes.

Pain Perdu

A great recipe for using leftover stale bread.

(serves 6-8)
1 baguette
225ml/8fl.oz unsweetened soya milk
50g/2oz vegan margarine
Sugar

1. Cut the baguette into slices approximately 3cm/1inch thick.
2. Dip the slices of bread in the soya milk until soaked through.
3. Squeeze each slice with care to remove excess milk and transfer to a plate.
4. Gently melt half the margarine in a large non-stick frying pan and fry the slices over a medium heat on each side until golden, adding the other half of the margarine before turning over. Remove from the heat.
5. Sprinkle with a little sugar and serve warm.

Sandwich Parisien

(makes 2)
1 baguette
2 large lettuce leaves
4 small slices of vegan ham
4 small gherkins, halved horizontally
Vegan margarine
Black pepper

1. Cut the baguette into two smaller sticks and cut each one open horizontally.
2. Spread the bottom half of each sandwich thinly with margarine and cover with a lettuce leave, with the lettuce slightly sticking out of the bread on the long side.
3. Place 2 slices of vegan ham in each sandwich. Garnish with the gherkins and season with black pepper.

Sandwich Provençal

(makes 2)
1 *poppy seed baguette* / classic baguette
4 tablespoons rocket leaves, chopped
2 tablespoons vegan grated parmesan
10 black olives, pitted and sliced
Olive oil

1. Cut the baguette into two smaller sticks and cut each one open horizontally.
2. Lightly drizzle the bottom half of each sandwich with olive oil.
3. Put the rocket leaves and sliced olives and sprinkle with the vegan parmesan.
4. Drizzle the crumb of the top halves with a little olive oil.
5. Place the open sandwiches under a hot grill for 10 minutes and close.

Sandwich Jardinier

(makes 4)
4 *petits pains*
1 carrot, grated
4 button mushrooms
4 tomato slices
1 tablespoon sunflower seeds
2 tablespoons grated celery
Soy sauce
French grainy mustard
Fresh chives, chopped

1. Cut each petit pain open horizontally.
2. Drizzle the soy sauce over the bottom half of each sandwich. Press the sunflower seeds in the crumb and cover with a thin layer of grated celery.
3. Slice the mushrooms and place them in a baking tray. Grill for 10 minutes.
4. Put the mushrooms over the celery and cover with a thin layer of grated carrot.
5. Place one slice of tomato over the carrot and sprinkle with fresh chives.
   Finally, spread the crumb of the top halves thinly with mustard.

Sandwich Sucré-Salé

(makes 2)
1 *sweet dough baguette*
4 cherry tomatoes, halved
2 dried apricots, chopped
2 tablespoons sultanas
2 teaspoons egg-free mayonnaise
2 large green cabbage leaves, shredded

1. Cut the baguette into two smaller sticks and cut each one open horizontally.
2. Spread 1 teaspoon egg-free mayonnaise over the bottom half of each sandwich. Sprinkle the sultanas and cover with shredded cabbage.
3. Place the cherry tomatoes on top and sprinkle with the chopped dried apricots.

Sandwich Rustique

(makes 2)
1 *pain épi* / wholemeal baguette
25g/1oz celeriac, peeled and grated
8 walnut halves
1 small apple, sliced thinly
25g/1oz cheddar-style "cheese"
Vegan margarine

1. Cut the pain épi / baguette into two smaller sticks and cut each one open horizontally.
2. Spread the bottom half of each sandwich thinly with margarine and put the cheese over it. Cover with the celeriac.
3. Put the apple slices in a pan and fry gently in a little margarine until soft.
4. Put the apples over the celeriac and place the walnut halves on top.

Pan Bagnat

(makes 2)
2 *sweet dough rolls*
1 tomato, sliced
2 lettuce leaves, shredded
4 teaspoons egg-free mayonnaise
1 tablespoon dried sea vegetables
Extra virgin olive oil

1. Soak the sea vegetables in a cup of water.
2. Meanwhile, prepare the pans bagnat. Cut both rolls in two horizontally.
3. Spread 1 teaspoon egg-free mayonnaise over each base and put the tomato slices on top.
4. Cover with the shredded lettuce and drizzle with olive oil.
5. Drain the sea vegetables and sprinkle over the lettuce.
6. Finally, spread 1 teaspoon egg-free mayonnaise on the crumb of each top and put the tops back over the filling.

Chocolate Tartine

(makes 2)
¼ baguette
8 small squares of vegan dark chocolate (approximately ¼ bar)
Vegan margarine

1. Cut the baguette into two horizontally.
2. Spread each half thinly with margarine and put 4 squares of chocolate over it.
3. Grill for 5 minutes.
4. Spread the melted chocolate over the tartine and serve warm.

Tapenade Tartine

Tapenade tartines are perfect served with a rocket salad.

(makes 2)
¼ *crusty seed baguette* / classic baguette
Tapenade:
50g/2oz black olives, pitted
1 tablespoon capers
1 plump garlic clove
2 tablespoons extra virgin olive oil
½ tablespoon lemon juice
Black pepper to taste

1. Blend all the ingredients for the tapenade.
2. Cut the baguette into two horizontally and spread each tartine with tapenade.

Tartine à l'Ancienne

(makes 2)
2 slices of *pain de campagne* / wholemeal bread
2 tablespoons vegan creamy "cheese" with herbs
1 tablespoon chopped walnuts
Vegan margarine

1. Spread the bread thinly with margarine, add the "cheese" and garnish with chopped walnuts.

Croque-Monsieur

(makes 2)
4 slices of *pain de mie* / white bread
2 ham-style vegetable slices
4 cheddar-style vegetable slices
2 tablespoons pasta tomato sauce
Vegan margarine

1. Spread each slice of bread thinly with margarine and put one slice of vegetable "cheddar", one slice of vegetable "ham" and another slice of "cheddar" on two of them.
2. Spread the pasta sauce over the "cheddar".
3. Put the remaining slices on top, margarine side up.
4. Place under a hot grill for 5-10 minutes and serve warm with a salad.

Sweet Croque-Madame

This sweet take on the *croque-monsieur* makes a perfect easy dessert or afternoon snack.

(makes 2)
4 slices of *pain de mie* / white bread
2 tablespoons raspberry jam
½ ripe peach, sliced
Vegan margarine
4 tablespoons firm silken-style plain tofu
1 tablespoon icing sugar
2 apricot halves in syrup, drained

1. Spread each slice of bread thinly with margarine.
2. Spread the raspberry jam on two of the slices and put the peach slices on top. Cover with the remaining slices of bread (margarine side down).
3. Blend the tofu and sugar until smooth and spread the mixture over the croque-Madames in a round shape, avoiding the corners.
4. Put the apricot halves on top, right in the middle.
5. Grill for 5-10 minutes and serve with a fresh soya yogurt.

Garlic Bread

(serves 4)
1 baguette
50g/2oz vegan margarine
3 plump garlic cloves, crushed
3 tablespoons chopped fresh parsley
1 teaspoon salt crystals
Black pepper to taste

1. Combine the margarine with the garlic, parsley, salt and pepper.
2. Cut the baguette into diagonal slices (approximately 2cm/1inch thick), making sure the slices are not entirely cut but still attached together at the base of the baguette.
3. Spread the garlic mixture between the slices of bread and grill the baguette for 10 minutes.

Croûtons

Traditionally served with onion soup, *croûtons* also make an ideal accompaniment to salads.

(serves 4)
1 *ficelle* / baguette
50g/2oz vegan margarine

1. Cut the ficelle into thin slices (approximately 1cm/½ inch).
2. Melt half of the margarine in a large frying pan and throw in the slices of bread.
3. Cover and fry gently on both sides until golden, adding the other half of the margarine before turning over.

Mouillettes

(serves 4)
½ baguette
Vegan margarine

1. Cut the baguette in half horizontally.
2. Spread the crumb thinly with margarine.
3. Cut each half into thin strips approximately 10cm/4inch long. Serve with hot soup, for dipping.

Dinner Party Canapés

An easy yet sophisticated starter for parties.

(serves 6)
6 slices of *pain de mie* / white bread
Toppings:
Vegan "cheese"
Vegetable paté
Tapenade (see *tapenade tartine*)
Harissa
Vegan margarine
Garnish:
Small gherkins, sliced
Capers
Pine nuts
Cherry tomatoes, halved

1. Cut each slice of bread into 4 equal squares.
2. Spread each square with one of the toppings, and add one of the ingredients for garnish, for example Vegan "cheese" and tomato, paté and gherkin, tapenade and pine nuts, etc.

DOUGHS AND CRÈMES

Rectangles of pâte feuilletée.

Introduction

The basic doughs presented here are the foundations of French sweet and savoury baking. Many of the pastries on offer in French pâtisseries are only variations on a few, incredibly versatile types of dough, and some national classics differ from each other only because of their shape, baking mode or filling. For example, a croissant and a pain au chocolat are very similar pastries, yet all pâtisseries in France will serve both. As for the éclair and the religieuse, which are regarded as distinct specialities, they are both puffs of choux pastry filled with crème and decorated with icing but shaped and assembled differently.

The types of dough below can be grouped in four basic types, each requiring a specific technique for a distinctive texture. Pâte levée is a soft dough leavened with yeast and is used in the preparation of soft cakes and pastries. Pâte feuilletée, or puff pastry, is made by folding the dough over margarine several times, making the dough rise in layers when baking. Pâte feuilletée will make rich pastries with a light crispy texture. Pâte brisée and pâte sablée are variations of shortcrust pastry and are mostly used for tarts and biscuits. They can be hard to handle but will make rich pastry with a crumbly texture. Finally, pâte à choux is cooked before it is baked, resulting in puffy hollow pastries. It is used in the preparation of individual puffs which are then filled with crème and can also be assembled into sumptuous desserts.

Because preparation of dough in general can be time-consuming, the recipes below usually make between 500g/1lb2oz and 1kg/2lb4oz of dough. One quantity can easily be used to make different recipes. Unleavened dough will keep well for a few days in the refrigerator, wrapped in cling film to prevent drying. It is preferable to freeze baked pastries rather than dough. Simply thaw in the refrigerator and warm the pastries through before serving.

Crème pâtissière and crème au beurre are two classics among the different creams used by the French pâtissier. Crème pâtissière is mostly used in fillings and will add a touch of vanilla to fruit pastries. Crème au beurre is a lot firmer and will set. It is a rich cream and therefore is ideal for piping into cake decorations. Tofu crème is lighter and makes a perfect filling or accompaniment to rich pastries.

Pâte Levée

(makes 950g/2lb2oz pastry)
500g/1lb2oz plain flour
100g/4oz caster sugar
1 rounded tablespoon dry yeast
300ml/10fl.oz soya milk, at room temperature
50g/2oz soft vegan margarine

1. Sift the flour and sugar into a large mixing bowl and mix in the yeast.
2. Form a well in the centre and pour in the soya milk. Add in the chopped margarine.
3. Combine with a wooden spoon. Knead into a ball, cover with a cloth and leave to rise for 2 hours.
4. Sprinkle the dough with flour and knead well.

Pâte levée cannot be kept refrigerated for more than one day. However, individual pastries can be frozen. Leave them out to thaw at room temperature before warming through in a hot oven.

Savoury Pâte Levée

(makes 900g/2lb pastry)
500g/1lb2oz plain flour
25g/1oz caster sugar
1 rounded tablespoon dry yeast
300ml/10fl.oz soya milk, at room temperature
50g/2oz soft vegan margarine

1. Sift the flour and sugar into a large mixing bowl and mix in the yeast.
2. Form a well in the centre and pour in the soya milk. Add in the chopped margarine.
3. Combine until soft and smooth and knead into a ball. Cover with a cloth and leave to rise for 2 hours.
4. Turn the dough out onto a floured surface and knead again. Add a little flour if necessary as the dough should be quite firm.

Because of the long waiting time, it is better to prepare one quantity of dough and use it up rather than divide the quantities. Pâte levée cannot be kept refrigerated for more than one day. However, the pastries can be kept frozen once baked.

Pâte Feuilletée (Puff Pastry)

Mille feuilles (middle) are prepared with pâte feuilletée.

(makes 1kg/2lb4oz pastry)
500g/1lb2oz plain flour
50g/2oz soft vegan margarine
250ml/9fl.oz cold water
250g/9oz hard vegan margarine, refrigerated
2 tablespoons cider vinegar

1. Sift the flour into a large mixing bowl.
2. Add the soft margarine and mix it in the flour with your fingertips until crumbly.
3. Pour in the vinegar, then gradually add the water while working the dough with your fingertips. Knead until smooth and firm, sprinkling with a little flour if necessary. Cover with cling film and refrigerate.
4. Wrap the hard margarine loosely in cling film and use a rolling pin to flatten it out into a rectangle approximately 1cm/½inch thick. Remove the film.
5. Turn out the dough onto a floured surface and knead firmly. The dough should be relatively firm, so add a little flour if it is too soft.
6. Roll out the dough into a rectangle twice the size of the margarine. Put the margarine over one half of the dough and fold the other side evenly over the margarine. Press lightly.
7. Roll out thinly. Fold both ends to meet in the centre then fold in two, forming four layers. Refrigerate for a couple of minutes.
8. Repeat step 7 three times, sprinkling the dough with a little flour if necessary.

Leftover dough can be kept refrigerated in cling film for a few days or frozen. Make sure that you keep it folded and do not shape it into a ball. Take it out of the fridge just before using.

Pâte Levée Feuilletée

A rich and light dough with a slightly crispy texture. This takes a little longer than *pâte feuilletée* to prepare but will make unique pastries. For a quicker option, you can replace by ordinary *pâte feuilletée* (puff pastry).

(makes 1kg/2lb4oz pastry)
500g/1lb2oz plain flour
15g/½oz caster sugar
50g/2oz soft vegan margarine
300ml/10fl.oz soya milk
1 rounded tablespoon dry yeast
250g/9oz hard vegan margarine

1. Sift the flour into a large mixing bowl and mix in the sugar and yeast. Form a well in the centre.
2. Cut the soft margarine into small pieces and place on the flour.
3. Heat the soya milk gently until lukewarm and pour it in the well.
4. Combine with a wooden spoon, then knead with hands.
5. Cover with a cloth and leave to rise for 1 hour 30 min.
6. Take the margarine out of the fridge. Wrap it loosely in cling film and use a rolling pin to flatten it out into a rectangle approximately 1cm/½in thick. Remove the film.
7. Turn out the dough onto a floured surface and knead well. The dough should be quite firm, so add a little flour if it is too soft.
8. Roll out the dough into a rectangle twice the size of the margarine. Put the margarine on one side of the dough and fold the other side evenly over the margarine. Press lightly.
9. Roll out thinly. Fold both ends to meet in the centre; fold in two forming four layers. Refrigerate for 5 minutes.
10. Repeat step 9 three times, sprinkling the dough with a little flour if necessary.

Pâte Levée Feuilletée can be frozen. Because it takes some time for a block of pastry to thaw, it is best to freeze the individual pastries when they are either ready to be baked or freshly-baked.

Pâte Brisée (shortcrust pastry)

(makes 500g/1lb2oz pastry)
200g/7oz soft vegan margarine, refrigerated
300g/10oz plain flour
3 tablespoons unsweetened soya milk
1 tablespoon caster sugar
1 teaspoon salt

1. Weigh all the ingredients and put in the fridge for 10 minutes.

2. Sift the flour and salt in a heap onto a work surface and form a well in the centre.
3. Put the soya milk and sugar into the well.
4. Chop the margarine and scatter onto the flour and sugar.
5. With a knife, work the margarine into the other ingredients until the mixture becomes granular.
6. Combine with your hands until smooth.
7. Form a ball and wrap with cling film, then put in the fridge until ready to use.

Pâte Sablée

Lunettes made with Pâte Sablée

Pâte Sablée must be prepared with cold hands so that the margarine does not melt before reaching the oven. Dip your hands in cold water before you start. If the pastry becomes sticky, put it in the fridge for 10 minutes but do not add flour.

(makes 600g/1lb5oz pastry)
100g/4oz caster sugar
200g/7oz hard vegan margarine, refrigerated
300g/10oz plain flour
5 tablespoons unsweetened soya milk

1. Weigh all the ingredients and put in the fridge for 10 minutes.
2. Sift the flour in a heap onto a work surface and form a well in the centre.
3. Put the sugar and soya milk into the well.
4. Dice the margarine and scatter onto the flour and sugar.
5. With a knife, work the margarine into the other ingredients until the mixture becomes granular.
6. Combine with cold hands until smooth, working as quickly as possible.
7. Form a ball and wrap with cling film, then put in the fridge.

When preparing biscuits or tarts with this dough, always work rapidly and with cold hands.

Wholemeal Pâte Sablée

(makes 600g/1lb5oz pastry)
100g/4oz caster sugar
200g/7oz hard vegan margarine, refrigerated
300g/10oz wholemeal flour
5 tablespoons unsweetened soya milk

1. Weigh all the ingredients and put in the fridge for 10 minutes.
2. Put the flour in a heap onto a work surface and form a well in the centre.
3. Put the sugar and soya milk into the well.
4. Dice the margarine and scatter onto the flour and sugar.
5. With a knife, work the margarine into the other ingredients until the mixture becomes granular.
6. Combine with cold hands until smooth, working as quickly as possible.
7. Form a ball and wrap with cling film, then put in the fridge.

Pâte à Choux (choux pastry)

(makes 600g/1lb5oz pastry)
350ml/12fl.oz water (250ml/8½fl.oz + 100ml/3½fl.oz)
25g/1oz vegan margarine
175g/6oz plain flour
100g/4oz potatoes, boiled, peeled and mashed
2 teaspoons baking powder
1 teaspoon sugar

1. Weigh all the ingredients and have them at hand, ready to be used. Mix together the flour and baking powder and set aside. Mix 100ml/3½fl.oz water to the mashed potatoes and set aside.
2. Put 250ml/8½fl.oz water, the margarine, salt and sugar in a large pan. Bring to the boil, stirring occasionally to melt the margarine.
3. Remove from the heat, add the flour mixed with the baking powder in one batch and combine with a spoon until the dough comes together and forms a smooth ball.
4. Cook over a low heat for 2 minutes while stirring occasionally.
5. Remove from the heat. With a food processor, hand-held mixer or wooden spoon, mix in half of the mashed potato mixture. Process until combined. Add the rest of the potato mixture and combine.

The dough is now ready to be used in recipes requiring pâte à choux.

Crème Pâtissière

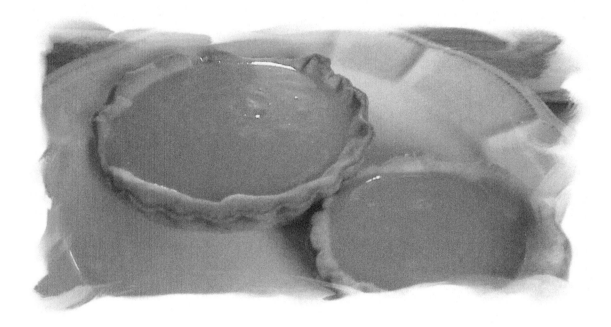

This vanilla-flavoured crème is a perfect filling for fruity barquettes. It is also used in the preparation of some classic tea-time pastries such as *escargots*. Leftover crème will make a delicious accompaniment to a dish of prepared fresh fruit.

50g/2oz soft vegan margarine
150g/5oz caster sugar
2 rounded tablespoons rice flour
150ml/5fl.oz soya milk
1 vanilla pod
2 teaspoons ground arrowroot

1. With a handheld mixer or food processor, cream the margarine and sugar together until soft and fluffy. Transfer to a mixing bowl.
2. Mix in the rice flour.
3. Slit the vanilla pod and scrape the seeds into the soya milk. Bring to the boil and add to the creamed margarine.
4. Combine and transfer the mixture back into the pan.
5. Add the ground arrowroot mixed with 1 tablespoon water and heat gently while whisking continuously. Bring to the boil (the mixture will start to thicken), remove from the heat and continue whisking for 2 minutes.
6. Sift into a bowl and leave at room temperature to cool. Crème patissière will keep in the refrigerator for a few days in an airtight container.

Crème au Beurre

Crème au beurre is a rich fluffy cream that is mostly used as a filling in cakes and individual pastries such as *Saint-Honoré* and *religieuses*. It will also keep its shape and therefore is ideal for piping into decorative swirls.

100g/4oz soft vegan margarine
325g/11oz icing sugar
1 tablespoon soya milk
Extra soya milk (up to 4 tablespoons)

1. Beat the margarine until soft and fluffy. Incorporate the icing sugar gradually and beat for 2 minutes. Add 1 tablespoon soya milk and beat again for 1 minute. Gradually add more soya milk while beating for a fluffier cream.

Crème au beurre will keep in the fridge for a few days in an airtight container. Beat vigorously before using.

Tofu Crème

350g/12oz firm silken-style plain tofu, drained
25g/1oz soft vegan margarine
1 tablespoon golden syrup
5 tablespoons icing sugar

1. Put all the ingredients in a food processor and blend until completely smooth. Transfer to a bowl, cover with cling film and refrigerate for 30 minutes. If not using immediately, whisk or blend again before filling pastries.

COFFEE TIME

Macarons

Introduction

The French love to round off family meals with a hot cup of freshly ground coffee served with a plate of biscuits. Some favourites are quickly prepared with leftover dough: a large tart can be made for dessert and baked in the same oven as some individual fruit *barquettes* to be served later with coffee. Strips of puff pastry quickly turn into crunchy *mini palmiers* or *chocolate twists*. Spices, dried fruit or nuts complement the aroma of the coffee. A colourful plate of *macarons* or *petits fours* is another refined choice, while melt-in-the-mouth *madeleines* are always popular. Biscuits are always best served fresh. If they are prepared in advance they will keep well in the fridge for up to a week, wrapped in cling film or in an airtight container. They can be warmed through before serving.

Macarons de Nancy

(makes 20)
Biscuits:
300g/10oz marzipan
125g/4½ rice flour
25ml/1fl.oz almond milk or soya milk
½ teaspoon baking powder
¼ teaspoon bicarbonate of soda
1 teaspoon almond extract
Filling:
90g/3½oz extra-firm tofu, drained
1 tablespoon soya milk
1 tablespoon golden syrup
½ tablespoon icing sugar
½ teaspoon almond extract
25g/1oz ground almonds

1. Dice the marzipan into a mixing bowl and add the rice flour, almond milk, baking powder, bicarbonate of soda and almond extract. Knead until soft and smooth.
2. Form the dough into a roll 2.5cm/1inch in diametre and cut into 40 slices approximately 1cm/½inch thick.
3. Carefully pat the slices along the edge to shape into round biscuits (without flattening out) and transfer onto a greased and floured baking sheet.
4. Bake in a preheated oven at 190°C/375°F/Gas mark 5 for 10 to 15 minutes until cracked on the surface and transfer immediately to a cooling rack.
5. Prepare the filling: put all the ingredients in a blender and blend until completely smooth.
6. Transfer to a bowl, cover with cling film and refrigerate for 30 minutes.
7. For each macaron, put ½ teaspoon of filling between 2 biscuits (flat side in) and press lightly.

Once filled, serve immediately. To keep for a few days, put the biscuits in an airtight container as soon as they have cooled and keep the filling separately in the fridge.

Macarons Chocolat

(makes 20)
Biscuits:
300g/10oz marzipan
125g/4½ rice flour
25ml/1fl.oz almond milk or soya milk
½ teaspoon baking powder
¼ teaspoon bicarbonate of soda
1 tablespoon cocoa powder

1 teaspoon chocolate extract
Filling:
90g/3½oz extra-firm plain tofu, drained
1 tablespoon soya milk
1 tablespoon golden syrup
½ tablespoon icing sugar
½ teaspoon chocolate extract
25g/1oz ground almonds
½ tablespoon cocoa powder

1. Follow the basic recipe for *Macarons de Nancy* (see above). For the biscuits, add the cocoa powder and chocolate extract to the marzipan mix. For the filling, add the chocolate extract and cocoa powder to the tofu mixture.

Macarons Rouges

(makes 20)
Biscuits:
300g/10oz marzipan
125g/4½ rice flour
25ml/1fl.oz almond milk or soya milk
½ teaspoon baking powder
¼ teaspoon bicarbonate of soda
1 teaspoon red food colouring
Filling:
90g/3½oz extra-firm tofu, drained
2 large strawberries
1 teaspoon strawberry jam
1 tablespoon soya milk
1 tablespoon golden syrup
½ tablespoon icing sugar
25g/1oz ground almonds

1. Follow the basic recipe for *Macarons de Nancy* (see above). For the biscuits, add the red food colouring. For the filling, put the strawberries and strawberry jam in the blender with the tofu mixture.

Madeleines de Commercy

Madeleine moulds
150g/5oz plain flour
125ml/5fl.oz soya milk
100g/4oz sugar
75g/3oz vegan margarine
1 teaspoon lemon juice
1 teaspoon baking powder
½ teaspoon bicarbonate of soda
¼ teaspoon salt
½ teaspoon vanilla extract
Extra vegan margarine

1. In a mixing bowl, whisk together the soya milk and lemon juice.
2. Gently melt the margarine in a pan and set aside to cool.
3. Meanwhile, sift together the flour, sugar, baking powder, bicarbonate of soda and salt into a large mixing bowl.
4. Stir the margarine into the soya milk mixture and add the vanilla extract.
5. Add the wet ingredients to the dry ingredients. Combine rapidly, then beat with an electric mixer for 15-30 seconds. Do not over stir.
6. Grease the madeleine moulds with margarine and fill them 3/4 of the way.
7. Bake the madeleines in a preheated oven at 175°C/350°F/Gas mark 4 for 15 minutes until golden.

Glacéed Cherry Biscuits

(makes 40)
300g/10oz *pâte sablée* (see *doughs and crèmes* section) / shortcrust pastry
50g/2oz plain flour
25g/1oz sugar
25g/1oz vegan margarine
20 glacéed cherries, halved

1. With your fingertips, mix together the flour, sugar and margarine in a bowl until crumbly. Put in the fridge.
2. On a floured surface roll out the pâte sablée into a rectangle 2mm/1/8inch thick.
3. Cut out approximately 40 small circles with a pastry cutter or upturned small cup, gathering and re-rolling the dough until used up. Transfer the biscuits onto a lightly greased baking sheet sprinkled with flour.
4. Take out the crumbly mixture from the fridge and scatter over the biscuits. Place one glacéed cherry half in the middle of each biscuit.
5. Bake in a preheated oven at 220°C/425°F/Gas Mark 7 for 10 minutes. Leave the biscuits on the baking sheet for a few minutes before transferring to a large serving dish.

Pink Hearts

(makes 40)
Heart-shaped pastry cutter
300g/10oz *pâte sablée* (see *doughs and crèmes* section) / shortcrust pastry
125g/4½oz icing sugar
50ml/2fl.oz beetroot or cranberry juice

1. On a floured surface roll out the pâte sablée into a rectangle 2mm/1/8inch thick.
2. With a heart-shaped pastry cutter, cut out approximately 40 biscuits, gathering and re-rolling the dough until used up and transfer onto a lightly greased and floured baking sheet.
3. Bake in a preheated oven at 220°C/425°F/Gas Mark 7 for 10 minutes.
4. Leave the biscuits on the baking sheet for a few minutes and transfer to a work surface.
5. Thin the beetroot or cranberry juice to intensify its colour by boiling it in a pan until there are only 3 tablespoons of juice left.
6. Put the icing sugar in a bowl and gradually add the juice until you obtain a thick and smooth paste. Spread over the cooled biscuits.

Blackcurrant Crowns

(makes 30)
Star-shaped pastry cutter
Round pastry cutter
500g/1lb2oz *pâte sablée* (see *doughs and crèmes* section) / shortcrust pastry
blackcurrant jam

1. On a floured surface roll out the pâte sablée into a rectangle 2mm/1/8inch thick.
2. With a round pastry cutter, cut out approximately 60 circles, gathering the dough and re-rolling it until used up. With a slightly smaller star-shaped cutter, cut out the centres of half of the circles. You can keep the cut out stars to make simple star-shaped biscuits or to use for *Icy Cinnamon Stars* (see below).
3. Transfer the biscuits (circles and hollow circles) to greased baking sheets sprinkled with flour and bake in a preheated oven at 220°C/425°F/Gas Mark 7 for 10 minutes.
4. Leave the biscuits on the baking sheet for a few minutes before transferring to a work surface.
5. Spread the jam over the biscuits without a hole and put the others on top.

Icy Cinnamon Stars

(makes 40)
Star-shaped pastry cutter
300g/10oz *pâte sablée* (see *doughs and crèmes* section) / shortcrust pastry
125g/4½oz icing sugar
½ teaspoon cinnamon
3 tablespoons water

1. On a floured surface roll out the pâte sablée into a rectangle 2mm/1/8inch thick.
2. With a star-shaped pastry cutter, cut out approximately 40 biscuits, gathering and re-rolling the dough until used up.
3. Transfer the biscuits to a lightly greased and floured baking sheet and bake in a preheated oven at 220°C/425°F/Gas Mark 7 for 10 minutes.
4. Leave the biscuits on the baking sheet for a few minutes before transferring to a work surface.
5. Mix the icing sugar with the water until you obtain a thick and smooth paste. Mix in the cinnamon and spread over the cooled stars.

Almond Diamonds

(makes 40)
500g/1lb2oz *pâte sablée* (see *doughs and crèmes* section) / shortcrust pastry
300g/10oz marzipan
20 blanched almonds

1. Slice the almonds in half horizontally and set aside.
2. On a floured surface and with a lightly floured rolling pin, roll out the pâte sablée into a rectangle approximately 2mm/1/8inch thick.
3. Roll out the marzipan into a rectangle half that size and carefully place the marzipan over one side of the pastry.
4. Cover the marzipan by folding the pastry over.
5. Transfer carefully to a greased and floured baking sheet and line the almonds on top, spaced out at regular intervals and slightly pressed in.
6. Bake in a preheated oven at 220°C/425°F/Gas Mark 7 for 12 minutes until golden.
7. Immediately after baking, cut approximately 40 diamonds from the rectangle, each with an almond in the middle (use a pizza cutter or sharp knife to cut crossing diagonals).

Strawberry Barquettes

(makes 14-16)
Barquettes moulds
500g/1lb2oz *pâte sablée* (see *doughs and crèmes* section) / shortcrust pastry
Vegan margarine
Filling:
1 quantity *crème patissière* (see *doughs and crèmes* section)
500g/1lb2oz strawberries, halved
Strawberry jam

1. On a floured surface roll out the pâte sablée into a rectangle 2mm/1/8inch thick and grease the barquettes moulds with margarine.
2. Lift the pastry into the barquettes moulds: roll the pastry around the rolling pin to lift it and carefully unroll over the moulds. Lightly press the pastry into the moulds with your fingertips and run the rolling pin firmly over the moulds to cut the individual barquettes. Prick the base of each barquette with a fork.
3. Bake the barquettes blind in a preheated oven at 200°C/400°F/Gas Mark 6 for 15 minutes. Leave the barquettes in the moulds for a few minutes before transferring to a cooling rack and leave to cool completely.
4. Put the crème in the barquettes, garnish with strawberries and glaze the strawberries with jam.

Barquettes are best consumed immediately. However, you can keep the empty barquettes in an airtight container and the cream in the fridge and assemble just before serving.

Easy Mandarine Barquettes

(makes 14-16)
Barquettes moulds
500g/1lb2oz *pâte sablée* (see *doughs and crèmes* section) / shortcrust pastry
Vegan margarine
Filling:
500g/1lb2oz mandarine segments in syrup, drained
Vegan whipped cream

1. Prepare and bake the barquettes as in the *strawberry barquettes* recipe (see above).
2. Fill the barquettes with the mandarines and pipe some cream on one side. Serve immediately or keep the empty barquettes in an airtight container and assemble just before serving.

Mango Cherry Creamy Barquettes

(makes 14-16)
Barquettes moulds
500g/1lb2oz *pâte sablée* (see *doughs and crèmes* section) / shortcrust pastry
Vegan margarine
Filling:
Crème au beurre (see *doughs and crèmes* section)
2 fresh mangoes, peeled and sliced
25 fresh cherries, pitted and halved

1. Prepare and bake the barquettes as in the *strawberry barquettes* recipe (see above).
2. Fill the barquettes with the mango slices and pipe some crème au beurre on top. Garnish with the cherries.

Serve immediately or keep the empty barquettes in an airtight container and keep the cream refrigerated. Assemble just before serving.

Spéculos

(serves 8)
1 sculpted biscuit mould (wooden is best), approximately 1cm/½inch deep
500g/1lb2oz plain flour
200g/7oz muscovado sugar / fine cane sugar
50g/2oz ground hazelnuts
50g/2oz ground walnuts
¼ teaspoon ground allspice
¼ teaspoon ground cardamom

1 teaspoon ground cinnamon
200g/7oz vegan margarine
75ml/3oz soya milk

1. Sift the flour into a large mixing bowl and form a well in the centre.
2. Beat the muscovado sugar until powdery and put into the well. Add the ground hazelnuts and walnuts, spices and soya milk.
3. Chop the margarine and scatter onto the mixture.
4. Work the margarine into the other ingredients until the mixture becomes granular. Combine with your hands until smooth.
5. Form a ball with the dough and wrap it with cling film. Refrigerate for 10 minutes.
6. Fill the mould with cold water, then empty it. Sprinkle the mould with flour and turn it over to remove any excess.
7. Fill the mould with refrigerated dough, pressing in the dough firmly and evenly.
8. Turn the mould over and tap gently to invert the spéculo onto a greased and floured baking sheet. If necessary, carefully run a knife along the edge of the mould.
9. Repeat steps 7 and 8 until the pastry is used up and bake the spéculos in a preheated oven at 200°C/400°F/Gas mark 6 for 15-20 minutes until golden brown.

Noir et Blanc

(makes approximately 40)
300g/10oz plain flour
150g/5oz granulated sugar
150g/5oz hard vegan margarine, refrigerated
6 tablespoons soya milk
1 teaspoon cocoa powder

1. Sift the flour in a heap onto a work surface and form a well in the centre. Put the sugar and soya milk into the well.
2. Dice the margarine and scatter over the flour and sugar.
3. With a knife, work the margarine into the other ingredients until the mixture becomes granular.
4. Quickly combine with cold hands until smooth. Form the dough into a ball, wrap with cling film and put in the fridge for 10 minutes.
5. Cut 150g/5oz off the ball and put this back in the fridge. Divide the remaining dough in two and mix the cocoa powder into one half.
6. On a lightly floured surface, roll out both portions of dough (light and dark) into rectangles 9cm/3½inch wide (approximately ½cm/¼inch thick).
7. Brush a little water over the rectangle of light dough and cover with the rectangle of dark dough.
8. Cut out 9 identical strips (1 cm/½inch large).
9. Take the 150g/5oz portion of dough out of the fridge and roll it out thinly into a rectangle as long as the strips. (You will later use this rectangle to wrap the strips together in a roll). Brush with a little cold water.

10. On the rolled out dough, place three strips tightly side to side so as to form a chequered pattern (alternating light and dark). Brush lightly with water and place three other strips. Brush with water again and place another three strips on top.
11. Carefully wrap the strips in the rolled out dough.
12. With a pizza cutter or very sharp knife, carefully cut the roll into slices 1cm/½inch thick. Transfer to a plate and refrigerate. Meanwhile, preheat the oven to 200°C/400°F/Gas mark 6.
13. Put the biscuits onto a lightly greased and floured baking sheet and bake for 10 to 12 minutes. Leave on the sheet for a few minutes before serving.

Cherry and Almond Petits Fours

(makes 30)
300g/10oz *pâte sablée* (see *doughs and crèmes* section) / shortcrust pastry
50g/2oz sugar
50ml/2fl.oz soya cream
50g/2oz blanched almonds, finely chopped
1 tablespoon vegan margarine
75g/3oz glacéed cherries, finely chopped

1. Put the sugar in a pan with 1 tablespoon water and cook gently, stirring regularly, until the sugar is dissolved.
2. Remove from the heat and mix in the cream and margarine.
3. Mix in the chopped almonds and cherries and set aside.
4. On a floured surface, roll out the pâte sablée into a rectangle 2mm/1/8inch thick.
5. Transfer the pastry to a greased and floured baking sheet by rolling it around the rolling pin, then carefully lifting it onto the sheet. Prick the pastry at regular intervals with a fork.
6. Spread the cherry and almond mixture over the pastry and bake immediately in a pre-heated oven at 200°C/400°F/Gas Mark 6 for 15 minutes.

As soon as it comes out of the oven, cut approximately 30 squares with a pizza cutter or sharp knife and transfer carefully to a serving plate.

Mini Palmiers

(makes 30)
300g/10oz *pâte feuilletée* (see *doughs and crèmes* section) / puff pastry
50g/2oz caster sugar

1. Roll out the dough into a rectangle 15x30cm/6x12inch (approximately 2mm/1/8inch thick).
2. Brush a little water all over the dough and sprinkle the sugar evenly on the water.
3. Roll the two smaller edges tightly to meet in the centre and join together.
4. Wrap the roll in cling film, transfer to a plate and put in the fridge.
5. Preheat the oven to 220°C/425°F/Gas Mark 7.
6. Cut the roll into slices ½cm/¼ inch thick with a pizza cutter or sharp knife and lay the slices flat on a greased and floured baking sheet, spacing them out as they will spread.
7. Bake for 15 minutes until golden and immediately transfer to a plate.

Chocolate Twists

Chocolate twists are perfect served with a cup of hot chocolate.

(makes 12)
300g/10oz *pâte feuilletée* (see *doughs and crèmes* section) / puff pastry
1 level teaspoon cocoa powder
1 level tablespoon caster sugar

1. Roll out the dough into a rectangle 20x25cm/8x10inch (approximately 2mm/1/8inch thick). Brush a little water over half of the pastry (starting from one of the smaller edges) and sprinkle the sugar and cocoa powder evenly on the water.
2. Fold the other half of the pastry over the sugar and cocoa and press lightly with a spatula.
3. Cut long strips horizontally, each 1cm/½inch large.
4. Twist the strips tightly and transfer to a greased and floured baking sheet, pressing down the ends lightly onto the sheet. Space out the twists to allow for spreading.
5. Bake in a preheated oven at 220°C/425°F/Gas Mark 7 for 10-15 minutes until golden. Transfer to a plate.

TEA-TIME TREATS

Pains au chocolat.

Introduction

The *goûter*, an afternoon light meal, holds an important place in French families, especially those with children. It is more than just a snack, and most children, as well as some adults, will sit at the table at four or five o'clock to enjoy a sweet meal accompanied by a glass of fruit juice or, in the winter, a small bowl of hot chocolate. Some *goûters* consist simply of a piece of fresh baguette with chopped chocolate or jam. But it is very common to have a sweet pastry or *viennoiserie,* and because most French pupils finish school between four and five o'clock, they will often buy their *goûter* at the local *boulangerie* on their way home. *Croissants, pains au chocolat, escargots* or a bag of fragrant *chouquettes* are very popular, but seasonal celebrations bring their ephemeral treats: a *goûter* around Mardi Gras will often consist of a *beignet* (deep-fried piece of dough) or, in the south of France, a *bûgne de Lyon* or an *oreillon.* While *tarte au sucre* and *palmier* are classics enjoyed by both children and adults, *lunettes* and *bonhommes* especially appeal to young children because of their original shapes.

Croissants

Croissants are delicious served warm, filled with jam or chocolate spread, or simply sliced in half and spread thinly with vegan margarine. Day-old croissants will need to be warmed through or can be used to make *almond croissants* (see below) or *toasted croissants* (see *savoury pastries* section).

(makes 6)
500g/1lb2oz *pâte feuilletée* (see *doughs and crèmes* section) / ready-made puff pastry

1. On a floured surface roll out the dough into a rectangle 50x20cm/20X8inch.
2. Cut the dough into 6 triangles 12cm/5inch across the base and 20cm/8inch from tip to base, alternating tips and bases along the length of the dough.
3. Brush each triangle with water before rolling up from base to tip and shaping into a crescent.
4. Transfer the croissants to a floured baking sheet, spacing them out to allow for spreading.
5. Bake in a preheated oven at 200°C/400°F/Gas mark 6 for 20 minutes until golden brown.

Almond Croissants

This recipe works best with day-old plain *croissants*, so you can enjoy freshly baked *croissants* and use leftovers to make these traditional Parisian treats.

Day-old *croissants* (see above)
Marzipan
Almond flakes
Soft vegan margarine

Icing sugar

1. Slice the croissants in half and put a thin strip of marzipan on each of the bottom halves.
2. Put the top halves back, covering the marzipan.
3. Spread a little margarine thinly over the croissant and garnish with almond flakes.
4. Bake in a preheated oven at 200°C/400°F/Gas mark 6 for 10 minutes.
5. Sprinkle with icing sugar and serve warm.

Pains au Chocolat

(makes 10)
1kg/2lb4oz *Pâte levée feuilletée* (see *doughs and crèmes* section) / ready-made puff pastry
200g/7oz dark vegan chocolate (approximately 2 bars)
3 rounded tablespoons caster sugar
Melted vegan margarine for brushing
Extra sugar

1. Roll out the dough on a floured surface in a large rectangle (40x50cm/16x20inch). If this is too large for your work surface, work with half the dough at a time to make 2 rectangles (40x25cm/16x10inch).
2. From your rectangle(s), cut out 10 strips of dough, 5cm/2inch in width.
3. Place 2 squares of chocolate along each of the smaller sides of the strips.
4. Roll in both ends of each strip until they meet in the centre, turning over the squares of chocolate three times. Turn over each pain so that the flat side is on top.
5. Transfer to a greased baking sheet, leaving at least 1cm/½inch between two pains. Brush a little melted margarine on top and sprinkle with a little sugar.
6. Set the pains aside for 15 minutes in a warm, draught-free room.
7. Bake in a preheated oven at 200°C/400°F/Gas mark 6 for 20 minutes and serve warm.

Leftover pains au chocolat can be kept refrigerated for a maximum of two days and should be warmed through before serving.
NB: If using ordinary puff pastry instead of *pâte levée feuilletée*, do not leave the pastries to rise before baking. Also note that pastries prepared with puff pastry will bake a little faster, so you might not need the full baking time indicated in the recipe.

Pains Antillais

A French Caribbean version of the famous *pain au chocolat*.

(makes 10)
1kg/2lb4oz *pâte levée feuilletée* (see *doughs and crèmes* section) / ready-made puff pastry
200g/7oz dark vegan chocolate (approximately 2 bars)
2 large ripe bananas

3 rounded tablespoons unrefined cane sugar
1 teaspoon vanilla extract
1 teaspoon ground cardamom
Melted vegan margarine for brushing
Extra cane sugar

1. Roll out the dough on a floured surface in a large rectangle (approximately 40x50cm/16x20inch). If this is too large for your work surface, work with half the dough at a time to make 2 rectangles (40x25cm/16x10inch).
2. From your rectangle(s), cut out 10 strips of dough, 5cm/2inch in width.
3. Mash the banana with a fork. Beat in the sugar, vanilla extract and cardamom.
4. Spread out the banana mixture thinly over each strip of dough.
5. Place 2 squares of chocolate along each of the smaller sides of the strips.
6. Roll in both ends of each strip until they meet in the centre, turning over the squares of chocolate three times.
7. Turn over each pain so that the flat side is on top and transfer to a greased baking tray, leaving 1cm/½inch between two pains. Brush a little melted margarine on top and lightly sprinkle with more cane sugar.
8. Set the pains aside for 15 minutes in a warm, draught-free room.
9. Bake in a preheated oven at 200°C/400°F/Gas mark 6 for 25 minutes and serve warm.

Leftover pains antillais can be kept in the refrigerator for a maximum of two days and should be warmed through before serving.
NB: If using ordinary puff pastry instead of *pâte levée feuilletée*, do not leave the pastries to rise before baking. Also note that pastries prepared with puff pastry will bake a little faster, so you might not need the full baking time indicated in the recipe.

Apple Chaussons

(makes 6)
500g/1lb2oz *pâte levée feuilletée* (see *doughs and crèmes* section) / ready-made puff pastry
3 large apples
50g/2oz sultanas
3 rounded tablespoons demerara sugar
1 teaspoon ground cinnamon

1. Peel the apples, cut into small cubes and put in a large pan with 2 tablespoons water.
2. Cook over a medium heat for 10 minutes, stirring occasionally.
3. Remove from the heat and add the sultanas, sugar and cinnamon. Mix well, transfer to a mixing bowl and leave to cool completely.
4. Roll out the dough on a floured surface into a rectangle 2mm/1/8inch thick.
5. Cut six equal circles out of the dough and transfer to a floured baking sheet.
6. Put the apple filling over one half of each circle, avoiding the edges.
   Dampen the edges of the circles with water, fold the dough over the filling and press to seal.

7. Make a few shallow diagonal cuts in the top of the dough for each chausson and leave to rise for 15 minutes.

8. Bake in a preheated oven at 200°C/400°F/Gas mark 6 for 15-20 minutes until golden brown.

NB: If using ordinary puff pastry instead of *pâte levée feuilletée*, do not leave the pastries to rise before baking. Also note that pastries prepared with puff pastry will bake a little faster, so you might not need the full baking time indicated in the recipe.

Palmier

(makes 4)

500g/1lb2oz *pâte feuilletée* (see *doughs and crèmes* section) / ready-made puff pastry

Sugar for sprinkling

1. Roll out the dough into a rectangle 55X20cm/22X8inch. Brush with cold water and sprinkle with sugar.
2. Fold the rectangle in four horizontally into a smaller rectangle 55X5cm/22X2inch. Press lightly to flatten.
3. Dampen both sides of the dough with a little water. With a pizza cutter or sharp knife cut into four long strips.
4. For each strip, fold over 5cm/2inch of dough at each end and continue folding to meet in the centre.
5. Lay the palmiers flat on a greased baking sheet sprinkled with a little flour, leaving enough space for them to spread out. Brush with a little cold water and sprinkle with sugar.
6. Bake in a preheated oven at 220°C/425°F/Gas Mark 7 for 15-20 minutes until golden. Carefully transfer to a cooling rack.

Apricot Windmill

(makes 9)
300g/10oz *pâte feuilletée* (see *doughs and crèmes* section) / ready-made puff pastry
9 apricot halves in syrup, drained
5 tablespoons apricot jam
1 tablespoon sugar

1. Roll out the dough into a square 30x30cm/12x12inch.
2. Cut into nine smaller squares 10x10cm/4x4inch and transfer to a greased baking sheet.
3. For each square, do the following:
    Starting from the corners, make diagonal cuts in the dough towards the centre, avoiding the middle where the apricot will be. The corners are now split in two. For each "double corner", fold one half towards the middle of the square. Always fold the same half of the corners (left or right) so that each side of the square has one fold.
4. Place one apricot half in the middle of each square. The pastry should look like a windmill with 4 blades around the apricot.
5. Bake in a preheated oven at 220°C/425°F/Gas Mark 7 for 12 minutes until golden brown.
6. Put the apricot jam and the sugar in a pan and bring to the boil. Brush over the windmills as soon as they come out of the oven.

Bonhommes

Gingerbread man pastry cutter
Dough:
500g/1lb2oz plain flour
100g/4oz caster sugar
1 tablespoon dry yeast
200ml/7fl.oz soya milk, at room temperature
50g/2oz soft vegan margarine
Decoration:
Dairy-free chocolate chips
Dairy-free chocolate vermicelli
Vegan margarine for brushing
Sugar for sprinkling

1. Sift the flour and sugar into a large mixing bowl and mix in the yeast.
2. Form a well in the centre and pour in the soya milk. Add in the chopped margarine.
3. Combine with a wooden spoon and knead into a ball. Cover with a cloth and leave to rise for 2 hours.
4. Knead the dough again before turning out onto a floured surface. Roll out into a rectangle ½cm/¼inch thick.
5. With a pastry cutter cut out person-shaped pieces of dough and transfer to a floured baking sheet.
6. Spread a little margarine thinly over each piece of dough and sprinkle with sugar.
7. Decorate the body with vermicelli. Use chocolate chips to make buttons and eyes.
8. Leave the bonhommes to rise for 20 minutes.
9. Bake in a preheated oven at 190°C/375°F/Gas mark 5 for 15 minutes.

Escargots

(makes approximately 15)
950g/2lb2oz pâte levée (see doughs and crèmes section)
75g/3oz sultanas
50ml/2fl.oz dark rum
175g/6oz crème pâtissière (see doughs and crèmes section)

1. Put the rum and the raisins in a mixing bowl and leave to soak overnight. Drain the raisins.
2. On a well floured work surface, roll out the dough into a square ½cm/¼inch thick.
3. Spread the crème pâtissière evenly over the dough and scatter the raisins over the crème.
4. Carefully roll up the dough.
5. Slice the roll into pieces 2cm/¾inch wide and set flat 5cm/2inch apart on a well floured baking sheet.
6. Flatten the escargots carefully with the palm of your hand.

7. Leave to rise for 10 minutes.
8. Bake in a preheated oven at 220°C/425°F/Gas Mark 7 for 12-15 minutes until golden and transfer to a cooling rack.

Chocolate Escargots

(makes approximately 15)
950g/2lb2oz pâte levée (see doughs and crèmes section)
75g/3oz chocolate chips
1 tablespoon cocoa powder
175g/6oz crème pâtissière (see doughs and crèmes section)

1. Follow the recipe for escargots (see above), replacing the soaked raisins with the chocolate chips. Sprinkle the cocoa powder over the crème.

Red Praline Escargots

A plate of freshly baked red praline

(makes approximately 15)
950g/2lb2oz pâte levée (see doughs and crèmes section)
175g/6oz crème pâtissière (see doughs and crèmes section)
Red praline:
200g/7oz raw peanuts
150g/5oz granulated sugar
60ml/2½fl.oz water
1 teaspoon red food colouring
½ teaspoon salt

1. First, prepare the red praline. Preheat the oven to 150°C/300°F/Gas mark 2.
2. Mix the sugar, salt, water and red food colouring together in a saucepan. Add the peanuts.
3. Cook the mixture over a medium heat, stirring regularly until the liquid is almost gone.
4. Use a spatula to spread the candied peanuts on a large baking sheet lined with baking paper.
5. Bake for 20 minutes without stirring.
6. Leave to cool completely on the sheet. Lift the paper off the sheet and break apart any large clusters.
7. Now prepare the escargots. Follow the basic recipe (see above) and replace the soaked raisins with the red praline.

Tarte au Sucre

(makes 6)
950g/2lb2oz pâte levée (see doughs and crèmes section)
50g/2oz vegan margarine
6 tablespoons sugar

1. On a floured surface, roll the dough into a stick and slice it into six equal portions.
2. Roll out each portion of dough into a circle ½cm/¼inch thick and transfer to a floured baking sheet.
3. Drizzle the dough with a little cold water. Chop the margarine into very small pieces and place them evenly over the dough. Sprinkle with the sugar.
4. Leave to rise for 30 minutes.
5. Bake in a preheated oven at 200°C/400°F/Gas mark 6 for 15-20 minutes.

Jam Beignets

Beignets are deep-fried in very hot oil (180°C/355°F), so make sure that the oil has reached the right temperature. You can test it by dipping a wooden spoon. Bubbles should appear around the spoon when the oil is hot enough. Do not cook too many beignets at a time or the temperature of the oil will drop, resulting in soggy beignets.

(makes 12-15)
950g/2lb2oz pâte levée (see doughs and crèmes section)
Jam (strawberry / apricot / raspberry)
Icing sugar

1. On a floured surface, roll the dough out into a square 40X40cm/16X16inch.
2. Use an upturned cup or a pastry cutter to cut out 24-30 circles approximately 8cm/3inch in diametre.
3. Put a teaspoon of jam in the centre of half of the circles, avoiding the edge. Brush the edge with water.
4. Cover with the remaining circles of dough and press firmly on the edges to seal. Leave to rise for 10 minutes.
5. Deep-fry the beignets in several batches for a few minutes until golden brown on both sides (turning them over once).
6. Transfer to a plate lined with kitchen roll and sprinkle with icing sugar.

Alternatively, replace the jam with dairy-free chocolate spread or chopped chocolate.

Oreillons

These soft beignets are called oreillons because they recall the shape of pillows ("oreillers" in French). Test the temperature of the oil with a deep-fry thermometer or a wooden spoon: bubbles appear around the spoon when the oil has reached 180°C/355°F. Also, never cook too many at a time or the temperature of the oil will drop.

(makes 60 small pieces)
950g/2lb2oz pâte levée (see doughs and crèmes section)
Icing sugar

1. On a floured surface, roll out the dough into a square 40X40cm/16X16inch.
2. Cut squares approximately 5X5cm/2X2inch. Leave to rise for 10 minutes.
3. Deep-fry the oreillons in small batches for a few minutes at 180°C/355°F, turning over once, until golden brown on both sides.
4. Transfer to a plate lined with kitchen roll and sprinkle with icing sugar.

Bugnes de Lyon

Before deep-frying the bugnes test the temperature of the oil with a deep-fry thermometer or a wooden spoon (bubbles appear around the spoon when the oil has reached the right temperature). Also, never cook too many at a time or the temperature of the oil will drop.

(makes 25)
500g/1lb2oz plain flour
100g/4oz caster sugar
300ml/10fl.oz soya milk
50g/2oz soft vegan margarine
Caster sugar

1. Sift the flour and sugar into a large mixing bowl.
2. Form a well in the centre and pour in the soya milk. Add in the chopped margarine.
3. Combine with a wooden spoon. Knead into a ball, adding a little flour if the dough is too soft.
4. Turn the dough out onto a floured surface and roll out into a square 40X40cm/16X16inch. Sprinkle with a little flour.
5. Cut strips of dough approximately 20X3cm/8X1½inch.
6. Knot each strip once loosely.
7. Deep-fry in small batches at 180°C/355°F, turning over once, until golden brown.
8. Immediately transfer the bugnes to a plate sprinkled with caster sugar and roll them in the sugar while still hot.

Lunettes

A spectacle-shaped, double-layered biscuit filled with jam and very popular with children.

(makes 6)
600g/1lb5oz pâte sablée (see doughs and crèmes section)
Strawberry jam
Icing sugar

1. Sprinkle the ball of pastry with a little flour and roll out into a rectangle ½cm/¼inch thick.
2. With a large round pastry cutter or the rim of a cup dipped in a little flour cut out twelve discs approximately 10cm/4inch in diameter.
3. On six of the discs use a smaller pastry cutter or plastic bottle cap to cut out two "eyes" in the centre. These will be used as the top biscuits.
4. Place the twelve discs on a greased and lightly floured baking sheet and bake in a preheated oven at 200°C/400°F/Gas Mark 6 for 10 minutes. Carefully transfer to a cooling rack.
5. When the biscuits have cooled, spread a thin layer of jam on the six bottom discs.
6. Sprinkle the top biscuits with icing sugar and place them on the bottom biscuits so that the jam shows through the "eyes".

The lunettes are best enjoyed fresh as they tend to soften quickly but they will keep in the fridge for a few days in an airtight container.

Chouquettes

(makes 15-20)
350ml/12fl.oz water (250ml/8½fl.oz + 100ml/3½fl.oz)
25g/1oz vegan margarine
175g/6oz plain flour
100g/4oz potatoes, boiled, peeled and mashed
2 teaspoons baking powder
1 teaspoon sugar
Pinch salt
50g/2oz sugar cubes

1. Weigh all the ingredients and have them at hand, ready to be used. Mix together the flour and baking powder and set aside. Mix 100ml/3½fl.oz water to the mashed potatoes and set aside.
2. Put 250ml/8½fl.oz water, margarine, salt and 1 teaspoon sugar in a pan. Bring to the boil, stirring occasionally to melt the margarine.
3. Remove from the heat, add the flour mixed with the baking powder in one batch and combine with a spoon until the dough comes together and forms a smooth ball.
4. Cook over a low heat for 2 minutes while stirring occasionally.
5. Remove from the heat. With a food processor or hand-held mixer mix in half of the mashed potato mixture. Process until combined. Add the rest of the potato mixture and combine.
6. Crush the sugar cubes coarsely and mix in the cooled dough.
7. Use a teaspoon to make 15-20 round heaps of dough and transfer to a baking sheet lined with baking paper greased with margarine.
8. Bake in a preheated oven at 220°C/425°F/Gas mark 7 for 10 minutes until the puffs have risen slightly and are beginning to colour.
9. Lower the oven thermostat to 175°C/350°F/Gas mark 4 without opening the door. Bake for a further 30 minutes.
10. Turn off the oven, prop the door ajar with a wooden spoon and leave in the oven for 15 minutes. Transfer the chouquettes to a cooling rack.

SAVOURY PASTRIES

Quiche Lorraine

Introduction

It is not surprising that pastry should often find its way into the main course of a French meal. *Tourtes* and individual *tartelettes* as well as regional specialities of international reputation, like *quiche Lorraine* and *flammenküsche*, are a great way to enjoy fresh seasonal vegetables such as spinach, leek, onions or pumpkin. Pastry can also be an original and refined way to serve a dish, and *vol-au-vents*, *chaussons* and *friands* are just as eye-catching as they are delicious.

All pastries from this section use pâte brisée, pâte feuilletée and savoury pâte levée which can be found in the section on doughs and crèmes. Note that most of the following recipes can be prepared with several types of pastry, and the French will often use different pastries depending on local customs, family habits or simply personal tastes. Feel free to experiment once you have tried the basic recipe: all variations will have a specific texture and flavour.

Pâté en Croûte

(serves 4-6)
500g/1lb2oz pâte brisée (see doughs and crèmes section) / shortcrust pastry, refrigerated
200g/7oz mushrooms, finely chopped
100g/4oz dry textured vegetable protein
1 large onion, finely chopped
500ml/18fl.oz vegetable stock
1 tablespoon olive oil
3 rounded tablespoons fresh parsley, finely chopped
1 rounded tablespoon fresh dill, finely chopped
3 rounded tablespoons wholemeal flour

1. Gently fry the onion in a large pan with the olive oil until soft and brown. Add the mushrooms and fry over a medium heat for 5 more minutes, stirring occasionally.
2. Add in the vegetable stock and vegetable protein, mix well, cover and simmer for 5 minutes. Uncover and cook over a medium heat until all the liquid is gone.
3. Put the mixture in a food processor and blend into a purée. Transfer to a mixing bowl, mix in the parsley, dill and wholemeal flour and set aside.
4. On a floured surface roll out the pâte brisée into a rectangle ½cm/¼inch thick.
5. Carefully transfer the pastry onto a greased and floured baking sheet by wrapping it around the rolling pin before unrolling it on the sheet.
6. Put the filling over one half of the pastry, shaping it into a large sausage.
7. Fold the other half of the pastry over the filling, dampen the edges with water and seal. Trim neatly along the edges. Roll out the trimmings into long, thin strips of dough and cross across the crust.
8. Bake in a preheated oven at 190°C/375°F/Gas mark 5 for 25-30 minutes until golden brown. Leave a few minutes on the sheet before cutting and serve with soya cream.

Saucisson Brioché

(makes 6)
900g/2lb savoury pâte levée (see doughs and crèmes section)
6 vegetable sausages, cooked
French mustard

1. Roll out the dough on a floured surface into a rectangle approximately ½cm/¼inch thick and cut it into 6 smaller rectangles. Spread a thin layer of mustard over the rectangles, avoiding the edges.
2. Place 1 sausage on each rectangle, along one of the smaller edges. Fold the sides of the dough over the sausages, roll up and seal with a little water.
3. Transfer, seam side down, to a floured baking sheet. Leave to rise for 20 minutes.
4. Bake in a preheated oven at 190°C/375°F/Gas mark 5 for 20 minutes.

Serve warm with salad.

Cream and Carrot Friands

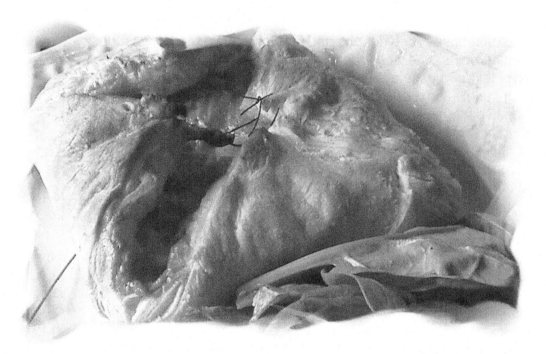

(serves 4)
500g/1lb2oz pâte feuilletée (see doughs and crèmes section) / ready-made puff pastry
300g/10oz carrots, peeled and finely chopped
100g/4oz potatoes, peeled and finely sliced
200ml/7fl.oz soya cream
1 tablespoon olive oil
2 teaspoons paprika
½ teaspoon cinnamon
½ teaspoon salt
Fresh parsley for garnish
Sprigs chive

1. Put the potatoes and carrots in a pan with the olive oil, cover and fry gently until the carrots are tender, stirring occasionally.
2. Add the soya cream, paprika, cinnamon and salt. Simmer, uncovered, for 5 minutes.
3. Remove from the heat and mash coarsely with a fork.
4. Roll out the pâte feuilletée on a floured surface into a square approximately 40X40cm/16X16inch and cut it into 4 smaller squares. Transfer to a floured baking sheet.
5. Divide the carrot and potato mixture into 4 and put each portion in the middle of one square of dough.
6. For each square fold the 4 corners over the filling, joining them together in the centre by threading two sprigs of chive through the corners with a needle. The friands should be securely joined so that the pastries will not open up during baking. Pinch on the sides to seal and make sure the pastries are joined.
7. Bake in a preheated oven at 190°C/375°F/Gas mark 5 for 20 minutes.
8. Garnish with fresh parsley and serve warm.

Spinach and Blue "Cheese" Chaussons

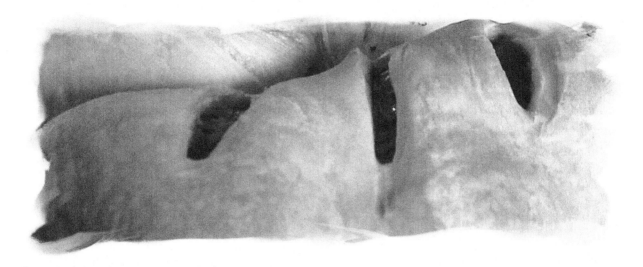

(serves 4)
500g/1lb2oz pâte feuilletée (see doughs and crèmes section) / ready-made puff pastry
200g/7oz fresh spinach leaves
150g/5oz blue-style dairy-free "cheese"
½ teaspoon black pepper
Fresh chives

1. Bring a large pan of water to the boil. Put in the spinach leaves and cook for 1 minute. Drain the leaves and set aside to cool.
2. Roll out the pâte feuilletée on a floured surface into a square approximately 40X40cm/16X16inch and cut it into 4 smaller squares.
3. Put the spinach leaves in the middle of the squares of dough. Add the pepper.
4. Divide the "cheese" into 4. Slice it thinly and put the slices over the spinach.
5. Fold the dough over the filling, bringing the sides together to overlap. Turn the pastries over and transfer to a floured baking sheet. Cut diagonal slits on top of each pastry.
6. Bake in a preheated oven at 190°C/375°F/Gas mark 5 for 20-25 minutes.
7. Serve warm, garnished with fresh chives.

Vol-au-Vents Jardiniers

(makes 8)
Vol-au-vent cases:
500g/1lb2oz pâte feuilletée (see doughs and crèmes section) / ready-made puff pastry
Filling:
100g/4oz cooked cut French beans, chopped
1 onion, finely chopped
50g/2 oz carrot, peeled and finely chopped
100g/4oz frozen soya mince
200ml/7fl.oz water
25ml/1fl.oz white wine
1 tablespoon olive oil
½ teaspoon salt

1. Gently fry the onions and carrots in the oil until soft.
2. Add in the soya mince and water. Simmer, uncovered, until all the liquid has been absorbed.
3. Add in the cooked beans and white wine and cook over a medium heat for 5 minutes. Stir in the salt. Remove from the heat and set aside.
4. Prepare the vol-au-vent cases: roll out the pâte feuilletée on a floured surface into a rectangle approximately ¾cm/1/3inch thick.
5. With a round pastry cutter or upturned cup, cut out 8 circles, each approximately 7cm/3inch in diametre. With a smaller pastry cutter or cup, cut out smaller circles (approximately 5cm/2inch) inside the 7cm/3inch circles so as to have 8 rings of dough.
6. Roll out thinly (2mm/1/8inch) the leftover dough and cut out 16 circles 7cm/3inch in diametre. Transfer these thin circles onto a greased and floured baking sheet.
7. Place the 8 rings of dough onto 8 thin circles, sealing with a little water. Do not flatten the rings. The last 8 circles will serve as tops for the cases once they are filled.
8. Bake the empty cases blind with the tops in a preheated oven at 200°C/400°F/Gas mark 6 for 10 minutes.
9. Transfer the vol-au-vent cases to a serving dish, heat the filling and fill up the cases before covering with the pastry tops. Serve warm with a glass of white wine.

Bouchées à la Reine

(makes 8)
Vol-au-vent cases:
500g/1lb2oz pâte feuilletée (see doughs and crèmes section) / ready-made puff pastry
Filling:
200g/7oz fresh mushrooms, finely chopped
150g/5oz shallots, finely chopped
50g/2oz chopped walnuts
2 tablespoons vegetable oil

2 tablespoons vegetable "gravy" powder
50ml/2fl.oz soya cream
25ml/1fl.oz water
Black pepper to taste

1. Put the walnuts in a large pan with 1 tablespoon oil and fry until fragrant and slightly roasted, stirring regularly.
2. Add the mushrooms, shallots and 1 tablespoon oil and fry gently until soft.
3. Pour in the water and stir in the vegetable "gravy" powder. Cook over a low heat until all the liquid is gone. Remove from the heat, add the black pepper and soya cream and set aside.
4. Prepare the vol-au-vent cases: roll out the pâte feuilletée on a floured surface into a rectangle approximately ¾cm/1/3inch thick.
5. With a round pastry cutter or upturned cup, cut out 8 circles, each approximately 7cm/3inch in diametre. With a smaller pastry cutter or cup, cut out smaller circles (approximately 5cm/2inch) inside the 7cm/3inch circles so as to have 8 rings of dough.
6. Roll out thinly (2mm/1/8inch) the leftover dough and cut out 16 circles 7cm/3inch in diametre. Transfer these thin circles onto a greased and floured baking sheet.
7. Place the 8 rings of dough onto 8 thin circles, sealing with a little water. Do not flatten the rings. The remaining 8 circles will serve as tops for the cases when they are filled.
8. Bake the empty cases blind with the tops in a preheated oven at 200°C/400°F/Gas mark 6 for 10 minutes.
9. Transfer the vol-au-vent cases to a serving dish, heat the filling and fill up the cases before covering with the pastry tops. Drizzle slightly with soya cream and serve warm.

Toasted Croissants

A great recipe for using leftover croissants

(serves 4)
4 croissants (see tea-time treats section)
4 ham-style vegetable slices
4 cheddar-style vegetable slices
50ml/2fl.oz soya cream
Black pepper to taste
Garnish:
Chicory leaves

1. Cut the croissants open and spread the soya cream evenly over the crumb.
2. Put half a ham-style slice and half a cheddar-style slice over each half croissant.
3. Add the black pepper and place under a hot grill for 5 minutes.
4. Serve warm with a salad of chicory leaves.

Quiche Lorraine

Quiche Lorraine is perfect with a glass of Moselle white wine.

(serves 4-6)
500g/1lb2oz pâte brisée (see doughs and crèmes section) / shortcrust pastry, refrigerated
300g/10oz firm silken-style plain tofu
100g/4oz vegetable rashers
3 large onions, finely chopped
25ml/fl.oz soya cream
1 tablespoon French mustard
1 tablespoon vegetable oil
1 tablespoon canola oil
1 teaspoon lemon juice
¼ teaspoon turmeric powder
½ teaspoon nutmeg
½ teaspoon salt
Pinch white pepper
Fresh parsley for garnish

1. Fry the onions in a large pan with the vegetable oil until soft and brown. Remove from the heat. Cut the vegetable rashers into small strips and add them to the onions. Set aside.
2. Put the tofu, mustard, lemon juice, canola oil, soya cream, turmeric powder, nutmeg and salt in a food processor and process until smooth and creamy. Transfer the mixture to another pan and set aside.
3. On a floured surface roll out the pâte brisée into a square approximately ½cm/¼inch thick and lift it into tart tin (of about 25cm/10inch diametre) lined with baking paper. Cut neatly around the tin.
4. Bake blind in a preheated oven at 190°C/375°F/Gas mark 5 for 15 minutes.
5. Meanwhile, cook the tofu mixture over a low heat for 5 minutes.

6. Put the onions over the pastry and cover evenly with the tofu mixture. Season with white pepper.
7. Bake at 190°C/375°F/Gas mark 5 for 25-30 minutes. Carefully lift from the tin and transfer to a serving dish. Serve warm garnished with fresh parsley.

Pâté Lorrain

(serves 4-6)
500g/1lb2oz pâte feuilletée (see doughs and crèmes section) / ready-made puff pastry
250g/9oz potatoes, peeled and finely diced
50g/2oz vegetable rashers
150ml/5fl.oz soya cream
25ml/1fl.oz white wine
1 large onion, finely chopped
2 shallots, finely chopped
1 plump garlic clove, finely chopped
2 tablespoons vegetable oil
1 rounded tablespoon finely chopped fresh chives
Pinch white pepper

1. Fry the onion, shallots and garlic in a pan with 1 tablespoon vegetable oil until soft and brown. Transfer to a mixing bowl, stir in the chives and set aside.
2. Put the potatoes in the pan with 1 tablespoon vegetable oil, cover and cook over a medium heat for 10 minutes, stirring occasionally to prevent sticking.
3. Pour in the soya cream and white whine and continue cooking, uncovered, over a low heat for 10 minutes.
4. Transfer to the mixing bowl, and add the ham-style slices cut into small strips. Add the white pepper. Mix well and set aside.
5. On a floured surface roll out the pâte feuilletée into a square 30X30cm/12X12inch.
6. Carefully transfer the pastry onto a greased and floured baking sheet.
7. Put the filling over one half of the pastry.
8. Fold the other half of the pastry over the filling; dampen the edges with water and seal. Trim neatly along the edges and cut a few slits on top of the crust.
9. Bake in a preheated oven at 190°C/375°F/Gas mark 5 for 25-30 minutes until golden brown. Transfer to a serving dish.

Leek Tourte

(serves 4-6)
400g/14oz pâte feuilletée (see doughs and crèmes section) / ready-made puff pastry
200g/7oz leeks, trimmed and sliced
200g/7oz braised tofu with its juice
100ml/4fl.oz soya cream

½ teaspoon white pepper

1. Fry the braised tofu in a pan for 10 minutes, stirring occasionally. Remove from the heat and set aside.
2. Put the leeks in a pan. Cover with water and bring to the boil. Reduce the heat and simmer for 10 minutes. Drain well and transfer to the pan with the tofu. Add the soya cream and cook over a low heat for 5 minutes while stirring occasionally. Remove from the heat and leave to cool completely
3. Cut half of the pastry and set aside. On a floured surface, roll out the other half into a circle approximately 2mm/1/8inch thick.
4. Lift the pastry into a tart tin (of approximately 25cm/10inch diametre) lined with baking paper and cut around the tin, allowing the pastry to overlap the tin by ½cm/¼inch.
5. Put the leek and tofu filling over the pastry and add the pepper.
6. Roll out the reserved portion of pastry into a circle approximately 2mm/1/8inch thick. Place the circle of pastry over the filling and pinch on the sides to seal like a pie, brushing with a little water to join.
7. Pile the trimmings of pastry on top of each other and roll out thinly. Cut out shapes for decoration (leaves, stars, circles, etc.) before placing onto the tourte.
8. Bake in a preheated oven at 190°C/375°F/Gas mark 5 for 35-40 minutes.

Spinach Tart

(serves 4-6)
300g/10oz pâte feuilletée (see doughs and crèmes section) / ready-made puff pastry
200g/7oz fresh spinach leaves
100g/4oz uncooked rice
350ml/12fl.oz water
2 tablespoons extra virgin olive oil
1 tablespoon lemon juice
½ teaspoon salt
Black pepper to taste
Soya cream

1. Put the rice in a pan with 350ml/12fl.oz water. Bring to the boil, reduce the heat and simmer until all the liquid has been absorbed.
2. Set aside a dozen spinach leaves for garnish. Bring a pan of water to the boil and cook the rest of the spinach for 1 minute. Drain the cooked leaves.
3. Put the rice and cooked spinach in a food processor and process until you obtain a thick purée. Stir in the olive oil, lemon juice, black pepper and salt.
4. On a floured surface, roll out the pastry into a square approximately 2mm/1/8inch thick and lift into a tart tin (of about 25cm/10inch diametre) lined with baking paper. Cut neatly around the tin and set aside the trimmings of pastry. Prick the pastry base all over with a fork.
5. Spread the spinach mixture over the pastry. Roll out the trimmings into long strips of dough approximately 1cm/½inch large and cross across the tart.
6. Bake in a preheated oven at 190°C/375°F/Gas mark 5 for 25-30 minutes. Serve warm, lightly drizzled with soya cream and garnished with fresh spinach leaves.

Onion Tart

This square tart prepared with pâte levée is ideal for buffets or dinner parties. You can make several tarts, varying the toppings, and serve the guests with an assortment of bite-size pieces.

(serves 6)
500g/1lb2oz savoury pâte levée (see doughs and crèmes section)
4 large onions
5 tablespoons tomato purée
2 tablespoons soya cream
1 tablespoon vegan margarine
1 teaspoon caster sugar
¼ teaspoon salt
1 teaspoon paprika

1. Slice the onions thinly.
2. In a large pan, gently melt the margarine and sugar together. Add in the onion slices, cover and cook until soft. Make sure you do not stir too much so that the slices do not come apart. Remove from the heat and set aside to cool.
3. In a bowl, mix the tomato purée with 5 tablespoons water and 2 tablespoons soya cream. Stir in the salt and paprika.
4. On a floured surface, roll out the dough into a square ½cm/¼inch thick and transfer to a floured baking sheet.
5. Spread the tomato paste over the pastry and cover evenly with the onion slices.
6. Leave to rise for 20 minutes.
7. Bake in a preheated oven at 190°C/375°F/Gas mark 5 for 30 minutes. Cut into rectangles or squares and serve either warm or at room temperature.

Flammenküsche

(serves 6)
300g/10oz savoury pâte levée (see doughs and crèmes section)
3 large onions
100g/4 oz baby potatoes with their skin, very thinly sliced
100g/4oz vegetable "rashers"
100ml/4fl.oz soya cream
1 tablespoon vegetable oil
Pinch white pepper

1. Slice the onions thinly and separate the rings.
2. Put the onions in a pan with the oil and fry for 15 minutes.
3. Cut the "rashers" into small strips, mix them with the onions and set aside.

4. On a floured surface, roll out the pâte levée into a large circle approximately 2mm/1/8inch thick and transfer to a floured baking sheet or pizza tray with air-flow system.
5. Spread the soya cream on the dough and put the potato slices over the cream.
6. Put the onions and rashers on top and season with the white pepper.
7. Leave to rise for 20 minutes.
8. Bake in a preheated oven at 190°C/375°F/Gas mark 5 for 20-25 minutes.

Carrot and Pepper Flamiche

(serves 6)
300g/10oz savoury pâte levée (see doughs and crèmes section)
250g/9oz carrots, peeled and grated
1 yellow pepper, finely sliced
1 garlic clove, crushed
100ml/4fl.oz soya cream
1 tablespoon vegetable oil
Pinch black pepper

1. Put the carrots and garlic in a pan with the oil and fry gently for 5 minutes, stirring occasionally. Set aside to cool.
2. On a floured surface, roll out the pâte levée into a large square approximately 2mm/1/8inch thick and transfer to a floured baking sheet or tray with air-flow system.
3. Spread the soya cream on the dough, add the carrots and place the pepper slices over the carrots. Add the black pepper.
4. Leave to rise for 20 minutes.
5. Bake in a preheated oven at 190°C/375°F/Gas mark 5 for 20-25 minutes.

Pumpkin Tartelettes

(makes 8-10)
Tartlet moulds
500g/1lb2oz pâte brisée (see doughs and crèmes section) / shortcrust pastry
500g/1lb2oz pumpkin flesh, finely chopped
150ml/5fl.oz soya cream
2 tablespoons pumpkin seed oil
4 tablespoons bread crumbs
Pinch white pepper
Vegan margarine

1. On a floured surface roll out the pâte brisée into a rectangle 2mm/1/8inch thick and grease the tartlet moulds with vegan margarine.
2. Lift the pastry into the tartlet moulds: roll the pastry around the rolling pin to lift it and carefully unroll over the moulds. Lightly press the pastry into the moulds with your fingertips and run the rolling pin firmly over the moulds to cut the individual tartelettes.
3. Put the pumpkin in a large pan with the oil, cover and fry gently until tender, stirring occasionally. Remove from the heat, add the soya cream and white pepper and mix well.
4. Fill the tartelettes with the pumpkin mixture and sprinkle with the bread crumbs. Put a small knob of vegan margarine over the bread crumbs.
5. Bake in a preheated oven at 200°C/400°F/Gas Mark 6 for 20-25 minutes.

Pissaladière

(serves 6)
300g/10oz savoury pâte levée (see doughs and crèmes section)
3 large onions, finely chopped
10 whole black olives
3 tablespoons olive oil
1 sheet sushi nori
½ tablespoon herbes de Provence
100ml/4fl.oz soya cream

1. Put the onions in a pan with 1 tablespoon olive oil, cover and fry over a medium heat until soft and brown, stirring occasionally. Set aside.
2. On a floured surface, roll out the pâte levée into a large circle approximately 2mm/1/8inch thick and transfer to a floured baking sheet or pizza tray with air-flow system. Brush the dough with 2 tablespoons olive oil.
3. Chop the sheet of sushi nori with a pair of scissors.
4. Mix the nori in the soya cream and spread over the dough. Add the onions, garnish with the black olives and sprinkle with the herbs.
5. Leave to rise for 15 minutes.
6. Bake in a preheated oven at 190°C/375°F/Gas mark 5 for 20-25 minutes.

Fresh Gondoles

(serves 6)
500g/1lb2oz savoury pâte levée (see doughs and crèmes section)
300g/10oz chopped tomatoes
2 large red onions, finely chopped
2 shallots, finely chopped
25g/1oz vegan margarine
3 plump garlic cloves, chopped
2 rounded teaspoons chopped fresh parsley
6 teaspoons extra virgin olive oil

1. Put the garlic, margarine and parsley in a bowl and combine. Set aside.
2. On a floured surface, roll the pâte levée into a sausage and slice into 6 equal portions.
3. With your fingertips, flatten out each portion into a long boat shape approximately ½cm/¼inch thick.
4. Transfer to a floured baking sheet and brush each gondole with 1 teaspoon olive oil.
5. Leave to rise for 15 minutes.
6. Bake in a preheated oven at 190°C/375°F/Gas mark 5 for 15-20 minutes. Immediately garnish with the chopped tomatoes, red onions and shallots. Put one knob of the garlic mixture on each gondole and serve before the base has cooled.

Mediterranean Flat Tart

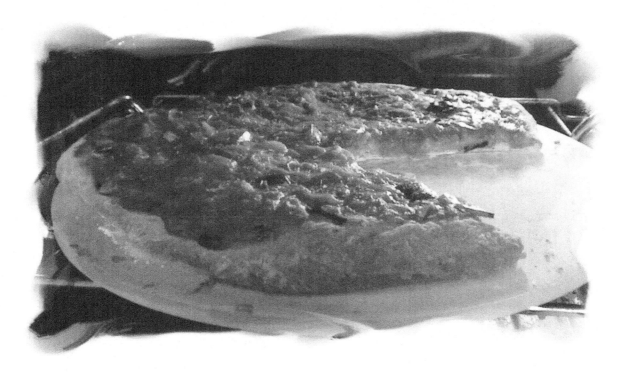

(serves 6-8)
Pizza stone or tray with air-flow system
500g/1lb2oz savoury pâte levée (see doughs and crèmes section)
400g/14oz ratatouille
1 tablespoon extra virgin olive oil
1 teaspoon dried thyme
1 teaspoon dried basil
1 teaspoon dried oregano
Pinch black pepper

1. On a floured work surface roll out the dough into a circle approximately ½cm/¼inch thick. Transfer to a floured pizza stone or tray.
2. Brush with the olive oil. Spread the ratatouille and sprinkle with the dried herbs and pepper.
3. Bake in a preheated oven at 190°C/375°F/Gas mark 5 for 30 minutes.

DESSERTS

Eclairs, religieuses and tartelettes.

Introduction

In France, both déjeuner and dîner -lunch and dinner- traditionally end with a dessert. At home, at work or at school, a meal would not be complete without a slice of cake, a small wedge of gâteau, or even an individual pastry such as a tartelette. Once again, local boulangeries-pâtisseries offer a wide range of desserts, from very simple easy options to the most elaborate desserts for formal family meals and special occasions. Home-baking is very popular in France and most people enjoy preparing in their own kitchen the classics of French traditional pâtisserie.

Fruit tartes and pies are an excellent way of using up leftover fruit from the garden, and the use of different pastries, fruit varieties, baking processes and garnish ingredients allows for varied combinations of flavours and textures. Quite a number of desserts have a regional origin·like the famous kouign amann from Brittany· and some ·like tarte tatin or baba au rhum· even have their own history. Seasonal desserts such as bûche de Noël or galette des rois are enjoyed throughout the country. It is also quite common to serve a selection of different individual pastries ·such as éclairs and mille-feuilles· from which guests can choose according to their tastes or appetite. As for special occasions, gâteaux are very often served at birthday parties while the spectacular croque-en-bouche nearly always crowns engagement parties and weddings.

Brioche

Brioche is delicious served warm with jam or simply on its own.

(serves 6-8)
Brioche mould or large cake tin
500g/1lb2oz plain flour
100g/4oz caster sugar
2 tablespoons dry yeast
½ teaspoon salt
350ml/12fl.oz soya milk, at room temperature
250g/9oz soft vegan margarine, at room temperature
50g/2oz flour

1. Sift the flour, sugar and salt into a large mixing bowl and mix in the yeast.
2. Form a well in the centre and pour in the soya milk. Add in 50g/2oz chopped margarine.
3. Combine until soft and smooth. Cover with a cloth and leave to rise for 2 hours.
4. Chop the remaining margarine (200g/7oz) and beat it vigorously into the dough with a wooden spoon until well combined and fluffy.
5. Roll the dough into a ball and transfer to a floured mixing bowl. Cover with a cloth and leave to rise for 1 hour.
6. Turn out the dough onto a well floured surface. Gradually incorporate 50g/2oz flour while kneading, until the dough comes together and forms a ball.

7. Transfer the ball to a brioche mould or cake tin greased with margarine.
8. Cover with a cloth and leave to rise for 30 minutes.
9. Bake in a preheated oven at 190°C/375°F/Gas mark 5 for 40-45 minutes.
10. Run a knife along the edge and leave in the mould for 10 minutes before transferring carefully to a serving dish.

Chinois

Chinois is a children's favourite and makes a great dessert with an original shape.

(serves 6-8)
Round cake tin at least 5cm/2inch deep
950g/2lb2oz pâte levée (see doughs and crèmes section)
Filling:
Crème patissière (see doughs and crèmes section)
Icing:
50g/2oz icing sugar
1 tablespoon water

1. Roll out the pâte levée on a floured surface into a square ½cm/¼inch thick.
    Spread the crème evenly over the dough and roll up.
2. Cut 4 to 5 thick slices from the roll and place them upright (spiral side up) next to each other in a deep floured cake tin. The slices should fill up the cake tin, so you can cut the roll into more slices if using a large tin.
3. Leave to rise for 10 minutes.
4. Bake in a preheated oven at 190°C/375°F/Gas mark 5 for 25-30 minutes. Leave to cool completely before preparing the icing.
5. Mix together in a bowl the icing sugar with 1 tablespoon water. Immediately decorate the cooled chinois with the icing and serve directly from the cake tin.

Candied Fruit Plait

(serves 6-8)
500g/1lb2oz plain flour
100g/4oz caster sugar
1 tablespoon dry yeast
200ml/7fl.oz soya milk, at room temperature
50g/2oz soft vegan margarine
100g/4oz mixed peel / crystallised fruit, chopped

1. Sift the flour and sugar into a large mixing bowl and mix in the yeast.
2. Form a well in the centre and pour in the soya milk. Add in the chopped margarine and mixed peel.
3. Combine with a wooden spoon and knead into a ball. It is normal to have a little excess flour in the bowl.
4. Cover with a cloth and leave to rise for 2 hours.
5. Knead the dough again and transfer to a floured surface. Divide into 3 equal portions and roll each one into a strand approximately 45cm/18inch long.
6. Weave the strands of dough tightly together into a plait and transfer to a greased baking sheet. Trim both ends of the plait.
7. Leave to rise for 30 minutes.
8. Bake in a preheated oven at 190°C/375°F/Gas mark 5 for 30 minutes. Serve with soya yoghurt or cream.

Bûche de Noël aux Noisettes

(serves 6-8)
950g/2lb2oz pâte levée (see doughs and crèmes section)
300g/10oz chopped hazelnuts
50g/2oz breadcrumbs
75g/3oz sugar
100ml/4fl.oz rum
Icing:
100g/4oz icing sugar
2 tablespoons water

1. Mix together the hazelnuts, breadcrumbs, sugar and rum in a large bowl.
2. Transfer the pâte levée to a floured surface and knead well. Add a little flour if the dough is too soft. Roll out into a rectangle 40X30cm/16X12inch.
3. Spread the hazelnut mixture evenly onto the dough and roll up starting from the longest side.
4. Transfer the roll, seam side down, to a floured baking sheet and leave to rise for 15 minutes.

5. With a pair of scissors cut small zigzags into the surface of the dough along the top of the bûche, leaving 2cm/1inch between two zigzags and at both ends.

6. Bake in a preheated oven at 190°C/375°F/Gas mark 5 for 35 minutes and leave to cool completely.

7. Prepare the icing by gradually mixing the water in the icing sugar until you obtain a thick paste and drizzle over the cooled bûche.

Pear Tart

(serves 6)
Dough:
250g/9oz wholemeal flour
50g/2oz caster sugar
1 tablespoon dry yeast
150ml/5fl.oz soya milk, at room temperature
25g/1oz soft vegan margarine
Filling:
3 pears
150ml/5fl.oz soya cream
50g/2oz rice flour
¼ teaspoon cinnamon
3 tablespoons demerara sugar

1. Put the flour and sugar together in a large bowl and mix in the yeast.
2. Form a well in the centre and pour in the soya milk. Add in the chopped margarine.
3. Combine with a wooden spoon. Knead into a ball, cover with a cloth and leave to rise for 2 hours.
4. Sprinkle the dough with flour and knead again.
5. On a floured surface, roll out the dough into a circle approximately 2mm/1/8inch thick and lift it into a floured tart tin.
6. Put the rice flour in a mixing bowl and whisk in the soya cream gradually. Add the cinnamon and whisk again.
7. Cut the pears in half and remove the skin and the cores.
8. Pour the soya cream mixture over the dough and place the pear halves in a circle, each pointing towards the centre of the tart.
9. Sprinkle the tart with the sugar and bake in a preheated oven at 190°C/375°F/Gas mark 5 for 25 minutes.

Galette des Rois

A favourite Epiphany tradition, the galette is a puff pastry pie filled with a rich almond crème. It is hugely popular in France and commonly served in the first few weeks of the year: a small figurine is hidden in the galette and the finder is crowned King or Queen in honour of the Magi.

(serves 8-10)
Large round tray with air-flow system (approximately 33cm/13inch)
If you wish to serve the galette for the Epiphany:
1 "fève" (small metal / ceramic figurine that is hidden in the almond crème)*
Paper crown: for the finder of the fève.
1kg/2lb4oz pâte feuilletée (see doughs and crèmes section) / ready-made puff pastry
300g/10oz vegan margarine
300g/10oz caster sugar
300g/10oz ground almonds
1 teaspoon almond extract
450g/1lb marzipan

1. Melt the margarine and beat in the sugar and ground almonds. Add the almond extract.
2. Cut the pastry into two equal blocks. Roll out one block on a floured surface into a large circle approximately ½cm/¼inch thick and transfer it to the floured round tray.
3. Roll out the marzipan into a slightly smaller circle and put it over the pastry.
4. Place the "fève" on the marzipan anywhere near the edge of the circle and spread out the almond crème over the marzipan.
5. Roll out the remaining block of pastry and cover the galette like a pie: brush the edges with a little water and press to seal.
6. Make shallow lattice cuts on the surface. Brush a little water on top and sprinkle lightly with sugar.
7. Bake in the middle of a preheated oven at 190°C/375°F/Gas Mark 5 for 35-40 minutes. If using a baking tray with air-flow system place another tray underneath as margarine may drip.

Make sure that you do not cut the galette in front of the guests. Bring the cut galette and let the youngest guest choose a share for everyone.
* Always be careful when biting into a piece of galette if using a fève. Do not serve to very young children.

Rhubarb Pie

(serves 6)
400g/14oz pâte feuilletée (see doughs and crème section) / ready-made puff pastry
400g/14oz rhubarb, peeled and chopped
150g/5oz demerara sugar

1. Cut half of the pastry and set aside. On a floured surface, roll out the rest of the pastry into a circle approximately 2mm/1/8inch thick.
2. Lift into a greased and floured tart tin (of approximately 25cm/10inch diametre) and cut neatly around the tin, allowing the pastry to overlap the tin by ½cm/¼inch.
3. Put the rhubarb over the pastry and sprinkle with the sugar.
4. Roll out the reserved portion of pastry into a circle approximately 2mm/1/8inch thick. Place it over the filling and pinch on the sides to seal the pie, brushing the pastry with a little water to join.
5. Bake in a preheated oven at 190°C/375°F/Gas mark 5 for 35-40 minutes.

Plum and Peach Tart

(serves 4-6)
300g/10oz wholemeal pâte sablée (see doughs and crèmes section) / shortcrust pastry, refrigerated
700g/1lb9oz small plums
2 tablespoons caster sugar
2-3 tablespoons peach jam

1. Cut the plums in half and remove the stones.
2. On a floured surface, roll out the pastry into a circle approximately 2mm/1/8inch thick and lift into a greased and floured tart tin (of approximately 25cm/10inch diametre).
3. Lay the plums, skin side down, over the pastry. Start along the edge, forming a circle with the plums, then lay a smaller circle inside, then another one until you reach the centre. Each circle should overlap the previous one a little.
4. Sprinkle the plums with the sugar and bake in a preheated oven at 200°C/400°F/Gas mark 6 for 35 minutes.
5. Fill the gaps between the fruit with peach jam and serve warm or at room temperature.

Tarte Tatin

The famous upside-down apple tart created by the Tatin sisters. This makes a refined and original dessert.

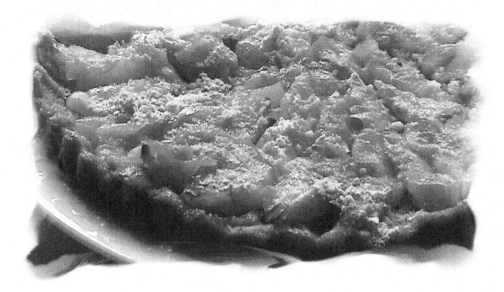

(serves 4-6)
300g/10oz wholemeal pâte sablée (see doughs and crèmes section) / shortcrust pastry, refrigerated
600g/1lb5oz apples
25g/1oz vegan margarine
2 tablespoons demerara sugar
Garnish:
Soya cream
2 tablespoons icing sugar

1. Cut the apples in half and remove the cores, leaving the skin. Cut into thin segments.
2. Put the sugar and margarine in a large pan and melt over a low heat. Add the apples and cook over a medium heat for 5 minutes, stirring carefully.
3. Arrange the apples neatly in a tart tin of approximately 25cm/10inch diametre greased with margarine. Start along the edge and arrange the apples in a circle (segments placed vertically and overlapping each other slightly), then form a smaller circle inside the first. Repeat until you have reached the centre and use any remaining apple to fill the gaps.
4. On a floured surface, roll out the pâte sablée into a circle approximately 2mm/¼inch thick to fit the tart tin.
5. Place the circle of pastry over the apples, cut neatly around the tin and tuck the pastry inside. Press down the pastry evenly over the apples and use the pastry trimmings to fill any large hollow on the surface.
6. Bake in a preheated oven at 175°C/350°F/Gas mark 4 for 45 minutes.
7. Invert the tart carefully onto a dish, sprinkle with the icing sugar and serve immediately, drizzled with a little soya cream.

Kiwi Tartelettes

(makes 8-10)
Tartlet moulds
500g/1lb2oz pâte sablée (see doughs and crèmes section) / ready-made shortcrust pastry
Vegan margarine
1 quantity crème pâtissière (see doughs and crèmes section)
10 kiwi fruits
Apricot jam

1. On a floured surface roll out the pâte sablée into a rectangle 2mm/1/8inch thick and grease the tartlet moulds with margarine.
2. Lift the pastry into the tartlet moulds: roll the pastry around the rolling pin and carefully unroll over the moulds. Lightly press the pastry into the moulds with your fingertips and run the rolling pin firmly over the moulds to cut the individual tartelettes. Prick the base of each tartelette with a fork.
3. Bake blind in a preheated oven at 200°C/400°F/Gas Mark 6 for 15 minutes and leave the tartelettes in the moulds for a few minutes before transferring to a cooling rack.
4. Peel the kiwi fruits and chop them into segments.
5. Put the crème patissière in the tartelettes and place the kiwi segments over the crème. Glaze the kiwi with apricot jam.

Lemon Tartelettes

(makes 8-10)
Tartlet moulds
500g/1lb2oz pâte sablée (see doughs and crèmes section) / ready-made shortcrust pastry
Vegan margarine
Lemon crème:
1 unwaxed lemon
50g/2oz soft vegan margarine
150g/5oz caster sugar
2 rounded tablespoons rice flour
125ml/4½fl.oz soya milk
2 teaspoons ground arrowroot

1. On a floured surface roll out the pâte sablée into a rectangle 2mm/1/8inch thick and grease the tartlet moulds with margarine.
2. Lift the pastry into the tartlet moulds: roll the pastry around the rolling pin and carefully unroll over the moulds. Lightly press the pastry into the moulds with your fingertips and run the rolling pin firmly over the moulds to cut the individual tartelettes. Prick the base of each tartelette with a fork.

3. Bake blind in a preheated oven at 200°C/400°F/Gas Mark 6 for 15 minutes and leave the tartelettes in the moulds for a few minutes before transferring to a cooling rack.
4. With a handheld mixer or food processor, cream the margarine and sugar together until soft and fluffy. Transfer to a mixing bowl.
5. Mix in the rice flour.
6. Bring the soya milk to the boil and add to the creamed margarine.
7. Combine and transfer the mixture back into the pan.
8. Add the ground arrowroot mixed with 1 tablespoon water and heat gently while whisking continuously. Bring to the boil, immediately remove from the heat and continue whisking for 2 minutes.
9. Sift into a bowl and leave at room temperature to cool. Grate the lemon peel and add it with the lemon juice to the crème. Mix well before filling the tartelettes.

Petits Choux

(makes 15-20)
Pâte à choux (see doughs and crèmes section)

1. Using a pastry bag pipe the pâte à choux into 15-20 round heaps of dough on a baking sheet lined with greased and floured baking paper. To pipe a chou, pipe a small spiral, starting with the middle and expanding into a round flat base, then start piping up, this time going from the edge towards the middle.
2. Bake in a preheated oven at 220°C/425°F/Gas mark 7 for 10 minutes until the puffs have risen slightly and are beginning to colour.
3. Lower the oven thermostat to 175°C/350°F/Gas mark 4 without opening the door. Bake the choux for a further 30 minutes.
4. Turn off the oven, prop the door ajar with a wooden spoon and leave in the oven for 15 minutes. Transfer the choux to a plate and leave to cool.

Vanilla, coffee and chocolate éclairs

(makes 6)
Pâte à choux (see doughs and crèmes section)
Filling:
Tofu crème (see doughs and crèmes section)
½ teaspoon vanilla extract
½ teaspoon extra dark liquid coffee
½ teaspoon coffee extract
1 teaspoon cocoa powder
½ teaspoon chocolate extract
Icing:
150g/5oz icing sugar

2 tablespoons water
1 tablespoon extra dark liquid coffee
1 teaspoon cocoa powder

1. Using a pastry bag pipe the pâte à choux into 6 balls of dough on a greased plate. Roll each heap into a smooth sausage approximately 15cm/6inch long and 2.5cm/1inch large. Flatten slightly into éclairs 3cm/1¼inch large. Transfer to a baking sheet lined with greased and floured baking paper. With a knife make a cut along both sides of each éclair.
2. Bake in a preheated oven at 220°C/425°F/Gas mark 7 for 15 minutes until the puffs have risen and are beginning to colour.
3. Lower the oven thermostat to 175°C/350°F/Gas mark 4 without opening the door. Bake the éclairs for a further 35 minutes.
4. Turn off the oven, prop the door ajar with a wooden spoon and leave in the oven for 15 minutes. Immediately remove the baking paper.
5. Prepare the filling: divide the tofu crème into 3 and transfer each portion into a small mixing bowl. Mix the vanilla extract in one portion, the coffee and coffee extract in another portion, and the cocoa powder and chocolate extract in the other portion.
6. Make a small hole at one end of each éclair and fill two éclairs with the vanilla crème, two with the coffee crème and two with the chocolate crème.
7. In a bowl mix 50g/2oz icing sugar gradually with 1 tablespoon water until you obtain a thick paste. Ice the two vanilla éclairs with a spatula. Mix 50g/2oz icing sugar with one tablespoon extra dark coffee and ice the two coffee éclairs . Mix 50g/2oz icing sugar with 1 tablespoon water, add 1 teaspoon cocoa powder and ice the two chocolate éclairs.

Religieuses

(makes 4)
Pâte à choux (see doughs and crèmes section)
Filling:
1 quantity crème au beurre (see doughs and crèmes section)
Icing:
100g/4oz icing sugar
2 tablespoons water
1 teaspoon cocoa powder

1. Reserve 1/3 of the pâte à choux and pipe the rest into 4 large puffs on a baking sheet lined with greased and floured baking paper. To pipe a chou, pipe a spiral, starting with the middle and expanding into a round flat base, then pipe up, this time going from the edge towards the middle, making the top flat. With a sharp knife make a shallow cut all around each puff.
2. Pipe the reserved portion of dough into 4 smaller heaps.
3. Bake in a preheated oven at 220°C/425°F/Gas mark 7 for 15 minutes until the puffs have risen and are beginning to colour.

4. Lower the oven thermostat to 175°C/350°F/Gas mark 4 without opening the door. Bake the choux for a further 35 minutes.
5. Turn off the oven, prop the door ajar with a wooden spoon and leave in the oven for 15 minutes. Immediately remove the baking paper.
6. Carefully make a small hole at the top of the big puffs and pipe crème au beurre inside. Fill the smaller puffs by the bottom. Reserve 4 tablespoons crème au beurre.
7. In a bowl mix the icing sugar and cocoa powder gradually with 2 tablespoons water.
8. Assemble the religieuses: spread some icing onto the big puffs, place the smaller puffs on top and ice. Pipe a ring of crème au beurre around the base of the small puffs.

Profiterolles

(serves 4)
12 petits choux (see above)
100g/4oz plain chocolate, chopped
75ml/3fl.oz soya milk
1 tablespoon golden syrup
12 small scoops dairy-free vanilla ice cream

1. Bring the soya milk to the boil over a medium heat. Remove from the heat, add the chopped chocolate and golden syrup and mix until smooth.
2. Carefully cut the petits choux open, place a small scoop of ice cream onto the bottom halves and place the choux tops over the ice cream.
3. Drizzle the warm chocolate over the choux and serve immediately.

Saint-Honoré

(serves 8)
200g/7oz pâte feuilletée (see doughs and crèmes section) / ready-made puff pastry
Pâte à choux (see doughs and crèmes section)
1 quantity crème pâtissière (see doughs and crèmes section)
1 quantity crème au beurre (see doughs and crèmes section)

1. On a floured surface roll out the pâte feuilletée into a neat circle of approximately 25cm/10inch diameter and transfer to a greased and floured baking sheet.
2. Pipe 150g/5oz choux pastry into a spiral (approximately 1cm/½inch thick) on the pastry base, starting from the centre and finishing right along the edge of the circle.
3. Bake in a preheated oven at 200°C/400°F/Gas mark 6 for 20-25 minutes. Transfer to a serving dish.
4. On a baking sheet lined with greased and floured baking paper, pipe the remaining choux pastry into 8 swirling puffs: for each puff pipe a spiral, starting with the middle and expanding into a round flat base, then start piping up, this time going from the edge towards the middle.
5. Bake the puffs in a preheated oven at 220°C/425°F/Gas mark 7 for 15 minutes until they have risen and coloured.
6. Lower the oven thermostat to 175°C/350°F/Gas mark 4 without opening the door. Bake the puffs for a further 25-30 minutes.
7. Turn off the oven, prop the door ajar with a wooden spoon and leave in the oven for 15 minutes. Immediately remove the baking paper and leave the puffs to cool.
8. Using a pastry bag, fill the inside of the spiral on the pastry base with crème au beurre. Reserve 2 tablespoons crème for assembling and garnish.
9. Carefully cut off the tips of each puff and set them aside. Fill the puffs with crème pâtissière. Garnish the top of each puff with a dollop of crème au beurre and put the tips back on.
10. Place the puffs around the edge of the circle, joining them to the base with crème au beurre. Do not cut the puffs when serving. Serve 1 whole puff per person.

Croque-en-Bouche

This elegant pièce montée, a pyramid of puffs on a base of nut brittle and covered with delicate caramel strands, is a popular dessert for weddings and celebration parties. This croque-en-bouche serves up to ten guests, but quantities can easily be increased to cater for larger parties.

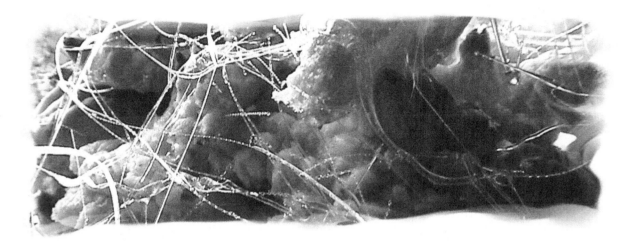

(serves 8-10)
30 petits choux (see above)
Nougatine base:
100g/4oz mixed nuts, very finely chopped
300g/10oz caster sugar
50ml/2fl.oz water
1 teaspoon lemon juice
Vegetable oil
Caramel:
150g/5oz caster sugar
25ml/1fl.oz water
½ teaspoon lemon juice

1. Place the chopped nuts in a tray under a hot grill until brown and fragrant, shaking the tray now and then to ensure even browning. Mix well and set aside to cool.
2. Line a round tart tin of approximately 23cm/9inch diameter with foil and grease with a little oil.
3. In a saucepan bring 300g/10oz caster sugar, 50ml/2fl.oz water and the lemon juice to the boil over a medium heat. Cook, stirring continuously until the caramel has reached 150°C/300°F. Reduce the heat and continue stirring until dark blonde. Immediately remove from the heat, quickly stir in the nuts and pour into the tart tin. Leave to cool completely before removing the foil and transfer to a flat serving dish sprinkled with caster sugar.
4. Bring 150g/5oz caster sugar to the boil with 25ml/1fl.oz water and ½ teaspoon lemon juice over a medium heat. Stir until the caramel has reached 150°C/300°F and turns a nice golden blonde. Remove from the heat.

5. Build the choux into a pyramid: dip the bottom of 12 choux in the caramel and place them on the nougatine base. Put another layer of 8 choux dipped in caramel. Build up 3 more layers of 5, 3 and 1 choux dipped in caramel. If the caramel becomes too sticky heat gently for a few seconds.

6. Before serving melt the remaining caramel over a low heat, remove from the heat and stir until it becomes sticky. With the tines of a fork, collect a small quantity of caramel and stretch it into thin strands between the puffs to decorate the pyramid. If the caramel becomes too hard reheat for a few seconds. Once the pyramid is decorated with caramel serve immediately.

Mille Feuilles

(makes 5)
500g/1lb2oz pâte feuilletée (see doughs and crèmes section) / ready-made puff pastry
Crème patissière (see doughs and crèmes section)
200g/7oz icing sugar
3 tablespoons water
½ teaspoon cocoa powder

1. On a floured surface roll out the pâte feuilletée into a rectangle 40X45cm/16X18inch. Cut into 3 smaller rectangles (40X15cm/16X6inch).
2. Transfer to greased and floured baking sheets. For each strip, cut 5 rectangles, each 8 cm/3inch wide. You should have 15 rectangles approximately 15X8 cm/6X3inch.
3. Prick each rectangle all over with a fork. This will ensure that the dough stays flat when rising.
4. Bake in a preheated oven at 220°C/425°F/Gas mark 7 for 10 minutes.
5. To assemble a mille-feuille, place one rectangle spread with a layer of crème patissière, cover with another rectangle spread with crème, and cover with a third rectangle. Do not spread crème onto the third rectangle. Set aside.
6. Put the icing sugar into a mixing bowl. Mix in the water gradually until you obtain a thick paste. Set aside 2 teaspoons icing and spread the rest generously onto the tops of the mille-feuilles.
7. Mix the cocoa powder in the remaining icing. Pipe thin parallel diagonal lines of the cocoa icing across the width of the white icing. Starting at one end, drag a wooden skewer across the cocoa lines to feather the cocoa icing. Repeat at regular intervals.

Three-Tier Cherry Cake

(serves 8)
300g/10oz pâte feuilletée (see doughs and crèmes section) / ready-made puff pastry
500g/1lb2oz cherries, pitted and halved
50g/2 oz sugar
1 teaspoon arrow-root powder
200g/7oz icing sugar
1 quantity crème au beurre (see doughs and crèmes section) / vegan whipped cream

1. Divide the pâte feuilletée into 3 and roll out each portion on a floured surface into a square 25X25cm/10X10inch.
2. For each square, use a round tin to cut out a neat circle approximately 25cm/10inch in diameter.
3. Transfer the three circles to greased and floured baking sheets.
4. Bake in a preheated oven at 220°C/425°F/Gas mark 7 for 7-8 minutes.
5. Put the cherries and sugar in a pan, cover and heat gently for 5 minutes until the juice has come out. Uncover and bring to the boil. Remove from the heat, put aside a few cherries for decoration and 3 tablespoons of the juice for the icing.
6. Mix the arrow-root powder with 1 teaspoon water and mix with the cherries. Bring to the boil and immediately remove from the heat.
7. Leave the cherry mixture to cool completely before spreading onto one of the circles in a flat serving dish.
8. Pipe a thin layer of crème onto the cherry mixture and cover with a circle. Pipe a thick layer of crème and cover with the last circle.
9. Prepare a pink icing by gradually mixing the reserved juice with the icing sugar until you obtain a thick paste.
10. Spread the icing onto the top circle, add a few dollops of crème and decorate with the reserved cherries.

Walnut Pralin Cake

(serves 8)
Fluted ring mould (of approximately 25cm/10inch diametre)
Pralin:
200g/7oz walnut pieces
150g/5oz granulated sugar
60ml/2½fl.oz water
½ teaspoon salt
Cake dough:
400g/14oz plain flour
300g/10oz caster sugar
200g/7oz soft vegan margarine
300ml/10fl.oz unsweetened soya milk

4 teaspoons baking powder
1 teaspoon bicarbonate of soda
Garnish:
Fresh white grapes

1. First, prepare the pralin. Mix the sugar, water and salt together in a saucepan. Add the walnut pieces.
2. Cook the mixture over a medium heat, stirring regularly until the liquid is almost gone.
3. Use a spatula to spread the candied walnuts on a large baking sheet lined with baking paper.
4. Bake the walnuts in a preheated oven at 150°C/300°F/Gas mark 2 for 20 minutes without stirring.
5. Leave to cool completely on the sheet. Break apart into small clusters.
6. With a food processor or hand-held mixer, cream the margarine and sugar together until soft and fluffy. Transfer to a large mixing bowl.
7. Sift in the flour, baking powder and bicarbonate of soda, add the soya milk and combine until no large lumps remain.
8. Stir in the walnut pralin.
9. Transfer to a fluted ring mould greased with margarine and use a spatula to flatten the surface of the dough. Bake in a preheated oven at 175°C/350°F/Gas mark 4 for 55-60 minutes until a skewer or knife comes out clean. Do not open the oven door before the first 50 minutes are over.
10. Leave the cake in the mould for 10 minutes before inverting onto a serving dish. Garnish the centre of the ring with fresh white grapes.

Marbré Breton

(serves 6)
200g/7oz plain flour
150g/5oz caster sugar
100g/4oz soft vegan margarine
150ml/5fl.oz soya milk
2 teaspoons baking powder
½ teaspoon bicarbonate of soda
2 tablespoons cocoa powder
½ teaspoon vanilla extract

1. With a food processor or hand-held mixer, cream the margarine and sugar together until soft and fluffy. Transfer to a mixing bowl.
2. Sift in the flour, baking powder and bicarbonate of soda, add the soya milk and combine until no large lumps remain.
3. Transfer half of the mixture to a mixing bowl and mix in the cocoa powder. Mix the vanilla extract into the other half of the mixture.

4. Grease a small loaf tin (approximately 1½litre/2½pint capacity) with margarine and pour half of the chocolate mixture into the tin. Then pour half of the vanilla mixture. Pour the rest of the mixtures, alternating colours as before.
5. Use a skewer or a knife to swirl in marble patterns.
6. Bake in a preheated oven at 175°C/350°F/Gas mark 4 for 45 minutes until a knife comes out clean.
7. Transfer to a cooling rack. Allow to cool for a few minutes if serving warm.

Kouign Amann

A soft flaky-textured cake from Brittany with a delicate tang of sea salt.

(serves 6-8)
500g/1lb2oz plain flour
300ml/10fl.oz water
2 tablespoons dry yeast
250g/9oz hard vegan margarine
250g/9oz caster sugar (150g/5oz + 100g/4oz)
1 teaspoon sea salt

1. Chop the hard margarine into a mixing bowl. Add in the salt and combine. Reshape into a block and refrigerate.
2. Put the flour and yeast together in a bowl and mix well. Form a well in the centre and pour in the water. Combine and knead into a ball. Cover with a cloth and leave to rise for 20 minutes.
3. Wrap the margarine loosely in cling film and roll out into a thick rectangle.
4. Turn out the dough onto a floured surface and knead quickly. Roll out into a rectangle twice the size of the margarine. Place the margarine over the centre of the dough and sprinkle 150g/5oz sugar over the margarine. Fold the dough over to enclose the margarine and sugar.
5. Stretch out the dough into a rectangle by pressing with your fingers.
6. Fold both ends to meet in the centre then fold in two, forming four layers. Leave for 20 minutes.
7. Roll out the dough into a rectangle, sprinkling lightly with flour if necessary, and repeat step 6 twice.
8. Transfer the dough into a large greased and floured tart tin and stretch out the dough with your fingers so that it fits in the tin.
9. Drizzle the surface of the dough with cold water and put 100g/4oz sugar evenly over the water. All the sugar should be absorbed.
10. Bake in a preheated oven at 190°C/375°F/Gas mark 5 for 30 minutes, placing a baking sheet underneath as margarine may drip. Serve with a bowl of Breton cider or cloudy apple juice.

Moka Truffle Gâteau

(serves 8)
400g/14oz plain flour
300g/10oz caster sugar
200g/7oz soft vegan margarine
300ml/10fl.oz unsweetened soya milk
4 teaspoons baking powder
1 teaspoon bicarbonate of soda
Moka mousse and garnish:
250g/9oz extra-firm tofu, drained and chopped
250g/9oz plain chocolate, chopped
50ml/2fl.oz unsweetened soya milk
1 tablespoon golden syrup
1 tablespoon instant coffee
1 teaspoon coffee extract
50g/2oz almonds, finely chopped
2 tablespoons cocoa powder
2 tablespoons icing sugar

1. With a food processor or hand-held mixer, cream the margarine and sugar together until soft and fluffy. Transfer to a mixing bowl.
2. Sift in the flour, baking powder and bicarbonate of soda, add the soya milk and combine until no large lumps remain.
3. Transfer to a deep round cake tin (of approximately 20cm/8inch diametre) greased with margarine and floured and use a spatula to flatten the surface. Bake in a preheated oven at 175°C/350°F/Gas mark 4 for 60-70 minutes until a skewer or knife comes out clean. Do not open the oven door before the 60 minutes are over.
4. Leave the cake in the tin for 10 minutes before transferring to a cooling rack. Leave overnight.
5. Put the tofu and golden syrup in a food processor. Heat the soya milk gently, add the coffee and stir until dissolved. Pour into the food processor. Add the coffee extract and blend all the ingredients until completely smooth. Set aside.
6. Put the chocolate in a double boiler or in a large bowl placed over a saucespan filled halfway with water. Bring the water to the boil, reduce the heat and leave the chocolate until melted, stirring occasionally. Remove from the heat and leave to cool for 3 minutes.
7. Put the chocolate in the food processor with the tofu mixture and blend until well combined. Transfer to a bowl, cover with cling film and refrigerate for 30 minutes.
8. Use a cake cutting wire or long sharp knife to slice the cake carefully in half horizontally. Trim the top if necessary. Spread half of the moka mousse onto the base and cover with the top. Spread 2/3 of the remaining mousse neatly over the top of the gâteau and refrigerate the rest of the mousse.
9. Place the chopped almonds under a hot grill until brown and fragrant and sprinkle onto the gâteau while still warm.

10. Divide the remaining mousse into 8 portions and roll each one into a small ball between the palms of your hands. Roll in the cocoa powder and place the truffles around the edge of the gâteau.
11. Sift the icing sugar over the almonds.

Cherry and Chocolate Gâteau

(serves 8)
400g/14oz plain flour
300g/10oz caster sugar
200g/7oz soft vegan margarine
300ml/10fl.oz unsweetened soya milk
4 tablespoons cocoa powder
4 teaspoons baking powder
1 teaspoon bicarbonate of soda
Filling:
200g/7oz griotte or dark cherry jam
Crème au beurre (see doughs and crèmes section)
8-10 whole cherries

1. With a food processor or hand-held mixer, cream the margarine and sugar together until soft and fluffy. Transfer to a mixing bowl.
2. Sift in the flour, cocoa powder, baking powder and bicarbonate of soda. Add the soya milk and combine until no large lumps remain.
3. Transfer to a deep round cake tin (of approximately 20cm/8inch diametre) greased with margarine and floured and use a spatula to flatten the surface. Bake in a preheated oven at 175°C/350°F/Gas mark 4 for 60-70 minutes until a skewer or knife comes out clean. Do not open the oven door before the 60 minutes are over.
4. Leave the cake in the tin for 10 minutes before transferring to a cooling rack. Leave overnight.
5. Use a cake cutting wire or long sharp knife to slice the cake carefully in three horizontally. If necessary, trim the top of the cake where uneven.

6. Spread half of the crème au beurre evenly onto the bottom circle and cover with another circle. Spread it with the cherry jam and cover with the last circle. With a spatula, spread the remaining crème au beurre neatly over the gâteau and garnish with the cherries.

Baba au Rhum

(serves 8-10)
Fluted ring mould (of approximately 25cm/10inch diametre)
Dough:
400g/14oz plain flour
75g/3oz caster sugar
1½ tablespoons dry yeast
350ml/12fl.oz soya milk, at room temperature
100g/4oz soft vegan margarine
100ml/4fl.oz dark rum
150g/5oz raisins
Glaze:
100g/4oz caster sugar
250ml/9floz water
100ml/4fl.oz dark rum
100g/4oz apricot jam
25ml/1fl.oz water
1 tablespoon sugar
Garnish:
300g/10oz fresh strawberries, chopped
1 tablespoon icing sugar

1. Put the rum and the raisins in a bowl and leave to soak overnight. Drain the raisins and keep any excess of rum for the glaze.
2. Sift the flour and sugar into a large mixing bowl and mix in the yeast.
3. Form a well in the centre and pour in the soya milk. Add in the chopped margarine and raisins.
4. Combine with a wooden spoon, cover with a cloth and leave to rise for 2 hours.
5. Beat the dough again before transferring to a fluted ring mould greased with margarine. Leave to rise for 15 minutes.
6. Bake in a preheated oven at 190°C/375°F/Gas mark 5 for 35 minutes. Leave the cake in the mould for 10 minutes before transferring, upside down, to a serving dish.
7. In a saucepan mix together the sugar and water and stir over a low heat until dissolved. Add the rum and spoon the mixture evenly over the warm cake. Pause every now and then to let the cake absorb all the liquid.
8. Put the apricot jam with 25ml/1fl.oz water and 1 tablespoon sugar in a pan. Bring to the boil, remove from the heat and spread over the cake.
9. Before serving, fill the hollow of the baba with the strawberries and sprinkle with the icing sugar.

ABOUT THE AUTHORS

Marianne and Jean-Michel are both French and vegans with a strong interest in animal rights and environment issues. They live with their three cats on the north coast of Scotland. They also write children's fiction and have already published a picture book for very young readers: Never Give Up, Bumble B (2008, Trafford Publishing). They are both nature lovers and enjoy drawing, playing music, dancing and reading Japanese manga.

In addition to writing, Marianne and Jean-Michel design unique handcrafted jewellery. You can see their collections and watch how the pieces are made on their website:

www.nezumiz.com

Marianne and Jean-Michel would love to know what you think about this book. Feel free to send them your comments and suggestions at **nezumiz@ymail.com.**

ALSO BY MARIANNE & JEAN-MICHEL

When Bumble is caught in a storm, he thinks he'll never be able to fly. A new friend will show him that with a little hope, anything is possible!

"An uplifting tale… beautifully and colourfully illustrated." The Northern Times

Never Give up, Bumble B.

Available from www.Trafford.com and all major online bookshops.

Made in the USA
Monee, IL
21 November 2020